# JACK KNOX:

## Learning Life's Lessons with Stock Dogs

ISBN 978-0-9600259-0-9
Cover designed by Emily Kitching.

# Contents

# *Acknowledgements*

Without encouragement from my friends right and left, this book would never have gotten past the thought state. Not only are Lora Withnell and Marilyn Volpe my good friends, they have been my guides, my encouragement, and my drive to keep writing when I was at a loss and ready to quit. I will always be grateful for all of their help and advice, even though, at times, it was questioned. The book has brought us together more than they will ever know. The ups and downs we shared have created, for me anyway, a sound friendship for life.

I'd also like to thank the people who come along when the challenges are too big for me: my family. Kathy and Kate, you may never know how much you have both added to this book. Whenever times were hard, a moment did not pass when I neglected to think about you both. Even though you may not believe it, you shed light on many issues for me and helped me solve them. Thank you, Kathy, for always being there for me. Your support and love is what gives me my strength to push forward and accomplish my goals. To you, Kate, your love, support and pride that you make me feel has had an everlasting effect on me.

To my daughters Jacqueline and Julie, their husbands Matt and Stuart and my grandkids Vivian, Glen, Evelyn, and Finlay; although you may not always think this way, you are my rock. You and all my family make me who I am and gave me strength as each word and paragraph was written. I hope you are as proud of me as I am of all of you. I feel blessed.

To all of my students and friends, thank you for giving so much. You, your dogs, your questions, and your answers have made this all possible. I hope in some small way, I have returned to you the joy and energy you have given me. I also hope that I have given you some answers as well.

# *Publisher's Note*

Jack Knox is an accomplished herding dog trainer. This book really is a conversation between Jack and the reader as he explains how dogs have shaped his life. In the course of Jack's stream of thought narrative, he uses terms that are commonplace to him and others who are familiar with the herding dog world. A handful of these words might trip up the reader who is uninitiated with herding dogs, so below is a quick glossary of terms to help those folks who are less familiar with working stock dogs.

**Trial**—a formal competition in which herding dogs work sheep (or cattle) on a course.

**Flank**—when the dog goes to the right or the left to control the livestock.

**Outrun**—the initial action when a dog is sent around one side of a group of stock to fetch them.

**Shed**—cutting one or more sheep out of a group.

**Recall**—indicating to a dog to leave the stock, quit herding, and return to the handler.

**Grip**—when a dog bites the stock.

**Lift**—the point after the outrun at which a dog gently picks up the livestock and begins to work them.

**Fetch gates**—gates that are situated on a trial course with openings between them so that dogs may herd the stock through them at points along the course.

# To Jackie Knox
# (The Ettrick Shepherd)

The sunrise breaks above the hills
The rosy glow lights up the rills
The sleepy Ettrick Valley stirs
'mongst rowans, beech, and Douglas firs

The curlew pipes her lonely cry
A blackie's heart sings out on high
As man and beast wake from their sleep
The shepherd climbs to check his sheep

With collies running at his side
He looks at them with love and pride
Their eyes are bright, so keen to please
As o'er the hill they move with ease

But on this bright and glorious day
The shepherd's thoughts are far away
To run his dogs he wants to be
In land so far across the sea

As time goes by, the hour draws near
To leave his Ettrick Valley dear
So to the States he takes his wife
And says farewell to the Valley life

In that far country he does well
His expertise begins to tell
The shepherd demonstrates his skill
Of running dogs on field and hill

Last year my memories flooded back
When once again I read of Jack
In the "Shepherd's Wife" I saw his name
By Viv, of Tweedhope Sheepdogs fame.

She mentioned a trip to the U.S.A.
And wrote of how she's been to stay
With Jack and his wife, on her trip out there
And how she'd enjoyed the American Fayre.

So I read with interest, your column today
On the Ettrick Shepherd, who went away,
Of a fairy tale which did come true
For a lad whom most of the valleys knew

No claim to fame will change this man
As sometimes fame and fortune can
But to us, as we steal along life's track
He'll still be the Ettrick shepherd, Jack

~Anonymous

# Chapter 1:

# The Making of a Young Shepherd

I was born in a little village named Greenlaw in Scotland near the Lammermuir hills in 1940. I spent my first seven years on a farm called Halliburton, which was five miles from Greenlaw back into the hills. It was a big arable hill farm, which had a lot of workers on it. There were two shepherds and there were four of five men who worked on the farm.

My father, at the time, was a grieve; a grieve was someone in charge of all the men who worked on the farm and was also in charge of the every day running of it. I can remember those were happy years. I spent many a day out in the fields or playing on the road, which wasn't a public road but instead a kind of private road. I would play in the sand and draw fields and pastures—and shepherd

The home where Jack was born and grew up in.
*Photo by Frances Dickman.*

sheep and run my dogs, all just in my mind. In my imagination, I'd go out and send my dog and gather a field and take the sheep to the pens.

Then I would work as a shepherd would do in the different chores that needed to be done with sheep throughout the year. I still often think of those days today, great learning and great opportunity. Naturally, if I got the opportunity to go with or follow the shepherds, I trampled behind them whenever I could, thinking I was the big man. I was a shepherd in my mind. I learned a lot just watching and following them.

I was seven years old when we left Halliburton moving on to a place called Bassendean farm, near the little town of Westruther. There my dad was farm grieve again, and it was more of an arable farm, mainly cropland fields with barley, oats, and potatoes. After two and a half years, we moved to a farm called Fens. At this time, my dad moved up to shepherd manager, as it was a smaller farm with cropland and sheep; it was fields rather than hills. This is where I did most of my school years. It was similar only I got the chance to do more with the sheep because my dad was in charge.

At Ettrick Shaws a young Jack (second from left) and friends pose for a photo.

In those days we used boxes to feed the sheep grain in the morning. These boxes were shaped in a V to keep the sheep from walking in them, however, if the boxes were left turned up, birds would go and try to eat in them and mess in them so the boxes needed to be turned upside down in the evening. I can always remember it was a big thrill for me at night to get the chance to turn the sheep feed boxes. I used to be allowed to go around the fields, turn the boxes and take a dog. One of the things I was told was, "you do not work the dog." So I did that many, many nights; taking that dog along with me and sitting and talking to him, thinking of what I could have done had I been allowed to work him.

I went to school at St. Boswells and from there went on to Newtown, which is only two miles further on. That is where I finished schooling. I left school when I was 15 and worked at home on a farm for just under a year. We got the local paper every week, and one week it had an ad for a young shepherd at Ettrick Shaws Farm. I was at my dad right away for me to apply for it. He said, "No, there is no use in you applying for it; you don't have the experience for something like that." It took a lot of persuasion from me to get him

**The cottage at the Fens farm where Jack spent most of his school days.** *Photo by Frances Dickman.*

to let me apply for the job, but, in the process, I did apply and ended up getting the job as a young shepherd.

I left home when I was 16 and went up to Ettrick. It was a hill farm that had three shepherds on three hirsells, which was a hill that each shepherd had and took care of. The hill that I had was named Caverslea, the second was named the Shaws Hill, and the third one was called Gildersgreen. I was a single shepherd and there were two married shepherds there. They also had a cattleman and two other people who worked doing the tractor work and other labor. It was about a mile back off the main Ettrick road, and when you began to climb it was pretty steep and fell back down into the farm. I was there for six years shepherding. I had about 700 ewes and the replacements, so over 800 sheep total on my hirsel. I can still remember the days when I used to take off to go to the hill and the feelings I had. How proud I was that I was able to go and do this. When I left home, my father got me my first dog, who was a four-year-old female named Dot. She wasn't registered but she was trained by a shepherd. I can always remember saying to my dad that I wasn't too happy about it because I wanted a younger dog. I can always

**Beginning work at the Fens. Jack on the left.**

remember him telling me, "You think you know everything but this dog will learn you." He said, "in fact it will learn you more than you ever knew." To be honest, he was one hundred percent right. Dot and I went through many rough and tough tumbles but what a dog she was! She did a great job for me and led me into other dogs, and it was at that time that I really got interested in dogs.

When I moved, there was no electricity in Ettrick Valley. It had to have been 1967 or 1968 when electricity came up to the Valley. There was no electricity and very few tractors in those days. I can remember in the wintertime sometimes spending days with shovels opening the roads after we were blocked in with snow. One or two days would go by and the wind would blow and the road would fill again and we would have to start all over. Then came the time when we got a loader for the tractor and that made it a little bit easier so we moved on to getting a snow plow. There was a lot of history to that place. There were a few balers in these days and at Ettrick Shaws we had an old stationary baler. We used a sweep on the front end of a tractor to push the hay cuttings to the baler where we pitchforked it into the hopper by hand. It was something pretty

**The cottage where Jack lived on Bassendean farm.**
*Photo by Frances Dickman.*

new to a lot of people. As time went on, the newer balers came and everything in life became easier.

I often tell stories about Ettrick Shaws because that was when I was in my teens and I loved to play soccer and badminton and carpet bowling. Each night of the week, there was something going on at Ettrick's Bridge, the little village that was four miles away. At that time, all I had was a bicycle and most of the time it would have a flat tire or something would be wrong with it. Many, many nights I would run to Ettrick's Bridge. I would run four miles to town and four miles back and I would never think about it. Often I'd run down the hill, take my shoes and socks off, wade through the water, and then run down the road till my feet were dry before putting my socks and shoes back on. I went down to play soccer and afterwards I went to the pub and had a pint then ran back home.

Along with that, my interest in training herding dogs grew more and more and I started going to watch trials. I must have been to at least a hundred trials before I even thought about running in one. I don't even remember where I was when I went to watch my first trial, but it was there that training dogs became more important to

**A view of Bassendean Farm.** *Photo by Frances Dickman.*

me. I would buy them for two or three pounds, would work them, and then sell them for six or seven pounds. This made a little extra money for me. I gained experience that led to where I am today. Jock Richardson was an acquaintance that became a good friend to me. Although he was never a mentor. I did talk to him a lot and I knew him pretty well. It is amazing what a guy can get from another if they see someone they like and watch and listen and ask little things. To me, I wish he was here today to tell him how much he has meant to me in my life. Another handler never educated me, but I got a lot of teaching through watching them and making up my own mind what I liked and what I didn't like.

I spent about six years at Ettrick Shaws and during these years, I remember when we used to shear. For example at shearing time, we would leave the house in the morning when it was dark, possibly 4:00 or 4:30 in the morning. We'd climb out onto the top of the hills and be ready to gather as soon as the daylight broke. We would come in with the sheep all gathered and in the pens ready to shear by 7:00 am. We would eat breakfast and then shear all day. It was nothing for 12-16 of us to be shearing sheep. It was all done by hand

**Caverslea hirsel at Ettrick Shaws where Jack started as a shepherd.**
*Photo by Frances Dickman.*

shears in those day and we would have people rolling the wool and putting it in the bags. Although it was hard work, it was fun times and I always looked forward to shearing.

Lambing time at Ettrick Shaws was also hard work. There were three shepherds lambing, and they always hired two lambing men so there would be five of us. There was always a kind of competition as to who was doing the best job. It was just a fun time to talk to people, to talk about their experiences with the sheep and the dogs. I used to leave early in the morning and I would make the first go round and be back in about 8:00 a.m. I would eat breakfast and then I would go back again and go out through all of the sheep and do anything that was left to be done; such as twining on lambs, taking ewes in that had lost a lamb, or checking other ewes that still had to lamb. I would have a break about midday, where I would get lunch between 1:00 and 2:00. We would have our break until 3:00 p.m. and then go away for the night round which would take us to roughly 7:30 in the evening. Then we would come back in and eat supper. Lots of really happy days were spent there and it's great to think back on some of these days.

**Jack in his first or second year as a shepherd in the pens at Caverslea selecting replacement lambs.**

When I left Ettrick Shaws, I started working what we called "working to your own hand" which means I was self-employed. I was shearing in the summer time and I drove livestock trucks for a while, I hauled hay and straw and did a little bit of this and that. The idea was, as a young guy, I wanted more money and like everybody else, thought money was the whole answer. At that time, I went to work for a company named Arnold's which was a truck contracting business hauling livestock and feed. I was with them for about two years. I think, honestly, the two years I was there, I always missed the sheep and the dogs and the lust and the pull for the hills and the heather, the work I really enjoyed. At the end of that time, I gave it up and I moved back and went to a place called East Deloraine as a young shepherd.

East Deloriane was a farm with about 1500 to 1800 acres, what we would term as one of the larger hirsals. We ran about 1100 Cheviot sheep on it. It was one of those places where you did a little bit of everything, tending cows included. It was a lonely type of life for me. I enjoyed my work, but it was in some ways too quiet, I liked being around people. It was a good experience and lots of things

**Entering the drive at Ettrick Shaws Farm.** *Photo by Frances Dickman.*

were learned while being there.

At East Deloraine, the ground closest to the road was very steep. When I got there one of the things I did notice was that the sheep hadn't been herded right. Back then, I was brought up being taught that the sheep should graze their way in from the hills tops in the morning and graze their way out in the afternoon and evenings. So I would go around the tops in the mornings to turn them in and around the bottom of the hill in the evening to turn them out. The sheep on the steep ground as I went to turn them in would run over the first knoll and hide. Then once I got to the bottom, I would look back and they had never gone any distance at all. They had stopped and were on their way back out. This annoyed me to the extent that I called my brother who was up near St. Mary's Loch and asked him if he had any, what I termed "rough dogs," dogs that would chase sheep and grab hold of them. They are not very good stoppers, but, at the least, they do go and chase the sheep. I borrowed two of his dogs and kept them for about three weeks. I used to take them when I went round the hill and send them after the sheep. I would just let

Looking onto East Deloraine Farm with the Ettrick River in the foreground. *Photo by Frances Dickman.*

them go and it did not take very long till, when I whistled as I went round the top in the morning, these sheep were on their way to the bottom.

There are a lot of messages in some of these stories if we would only stop and think. These sheep had been allowed to be lazy. Although they really wanted to get to better grazing, they were lazy and got half full and went and lay down. With a little bit of rougher dogging, as I would call it, or chasing, they began to think a bit more. As they thought, they started to stray and make their way to the top in the evening or the bottom in the morning the way we would expect good hill sheep to do. All you are doing by studying your sheep and understanding what they need is teaching them the right habits instead of the bad habits.

It's so interesting when I think back today on the dogs and sheep I've known, the trials and competitions of the past, and the questions that people ask and the answers they want. For example, why does a sheep not want to go into a pen? It could be the way you were trying

**Sign for East and West Deloraine Farms.** *Photo by Frances Dickman.*

to put it in the pen. Why does the sheep not want to go through the gates? It could be the way you are taking them to the gates. People often don't look to find that answer. Figure out what your sheep are thinking when you are having a problem; to me that is the best advice I could pass out to anybody, especially those wanting to trial. Don't always ask the questions, "how do I do this," or, "how do I do that?" Teach yourself to figure out what the sheep are thinking and they will give you the answer you need. A lot of that was taught to me during my shepherding years. I was on my own—I had nobody to tell me, so I just figured things out. I figured the easy way and the hard way. The hard way took longer and I didn't like that part.

I often think back on that today. Now-a-days, on the trial field, people want sheep that are dog trained, not sheep that are a challenge. To me, when you go to a dog trial, the sheep you draw is your packet to work.

I lambed inby, which is lambing in the pastures rather than the hills, for three years with my brother-in-law, Jack Kerr. To this day, I respect and have so much admiration for him and got an education that is still valuable for me even today. He was someone who was

**Looking across to East Deloriane from the Ettrick Valley road.**
*Photo by Frances Dickman.*

always very proud in what he did, and his number one passion was his sheep. He used to run about 700 Cheviot ewes, and I would go and help him lamb. The thing about Jack was, these sheep had to be right. If the sheep were not taken care of, everything else was left. That was his number one priority to the point that he knew every sheep individually. He could have told you a story about any sheep you pointed to. During the lambing while I was there, it just was invaluable to me, the things I learned through watching and him showing or telling me. An example was, most people during lambing time number or mark the twin lambs. Jack believed, "no you didn't put marks or numbers on them because well, look at them, you couldn't have that." He was a gifted man because he didn't need marks; he just knew lambs. I'm talking about baby lambs, maybe two or three days old and if there had been twenty of them there, he could have taken them all away from their mothers and then put them back and could have told you which lamb belonged to which mother. He was just amazing, what we call a Kenner. A Kenner is someone that knew his sheep well. I often tell a story about him: during my time there we took about forty pairs of ewes with twins, which is forty ewes and about eighty lambs. We were driving them up this highway about three quarters of a mile and were putting them into a field when his boss arrived. Jack was talking to his boss while I was in the field trying to mother up these forty ewes and eighty lambs. He was standing in the road saying to me, "See this one here, Jack? Take it over there; that's its mother," or "that one belongs with that mother over there." He knew every lamb and these lambs were only a few days old. To this day, that just blows my mind. It's something I'll never forget, something that was invaluable to me. It showed what you could do if you really enjoyed your livestock and treated them the way they should be treated.

Jack Kerr was never a man who was into dogs or trials or really training that much, but he did like a good dog. He liked a good dog and the reason was very simple: he didn't want a dog that was going to be abusing his sheep. But when he needed to do something with the sheep, he wanted a dog that he could handle correctly. He always had a good dog. I can always remember, he had a dog named Ben when I was there. Ben was some dog. He was just a really good everyday working dog and capable of doing anything you would ever need to do with sheep. Jack also had a bunch of young dogs and was one who didn't take the young dogs out too much because they would chase his sheep and abuse them. As a result, the young dogs never got the chance to develop as herding dogs. So I started, in the years later, taking some young dogs from him and training them. Some of them turned out pretty decent. Through doing all that, I became very interested in the dogs and ended up getting my first start in the registered Border Collies.

I got a young dog from Jack's brother, Ian, a puppy named Mist, who turned out pretty well. I trained her and as she came up she looked pretty good. Ian was over one day and saw her and said, "You should breed her to Wiston Cap." Of course many people know Wiston Cap was one of the most famous dogs that's ever been. I said, "Well, if you want to breed her to Wiston Cap, take her and

**Jack in his teens at Ettrick Shaws.**

get her bred. If you do that, we'll split the pups." So Ian took Mist and bred her to Wiston Cap and she had two puppies. These two puppies ended up being the start of a long and interesting sheep dog life for me. Their success took me into trials, took me to clinics, took me to America; it's all involved in the story.

The male puppy was named Bill and the female puppy was named Nan. I kept the female and started off with her. She turned out to be a topper, a really good dog. She was easy to train; she was my pride and joy. I used to take her out and train her and play with her. At seven months old, I had her fully trained. I could have done anything with Nan. She was the first dog I ever trialed. I first trialed her when she was about a year and a half old. She'd go on to be the first dog I ever won a trial with. Nan was something special. I wish I had Nan today.

On the other hand, Bill was the complete opposite. Ian had Bill and he was a stronger dog. When he was about ten months old, I got the chance to buy him back. Bill and I went through lots before I saw the real problem. He was a dog that, in my opinion, had been wrongly corrected and didn't understand his corrections. Through all that, it gave me a new insight into correcting dogs, studying dogs, and knowing what they needed and what they didn't need.

To start with, he used to dive, rip, and bite. I got rid of that, then he was quite nice on sheep. Bill got to where I couldn't recall him very well. One day, I was working in the corner of the field where we had stone walls which we called dikes in Scotland. I had the sheep up in the corner of the dike as I was working him and he wouldn't take his recall. As a result, I took my stick and hit the wall to make a noise, and call him off. Well, he saw the stick, he flew up over the wall and took off. He ran and hid and I hunted for him for about an hour, maybe longer. I finally found him cowering behind the stable door. When I found him I said, "Now I know your problem."

I started to work on that fear. As I worked on the fear, the dog got more confident and better; the trust between Bill and me started to grow. I would say Bill was possibly three by the time I finally got him trained to where I could run him. In the end he was some dog. Nan and Bill were the two dogs that accompanied me when I made my journey across the water to America.

# Chapter 2:

The Last Days in
Scotland

Gilmansleuch was the last farm I worked at before leaving the
United Kingdom for America. It was a hill place with about 1200
acres. It had about 200 acres of what we called inby ground, which
was field ground, and about 1000 acres on the hill. We ran about
1000 head of sheep and about 30 cows. I ended up shepherd
manager on that place for a man by the name of Robin Johnson.
Robin, who had started from scratch years ahead, owned three hill
farms and was just a great guy and another great asset to my life. He
gave me opportunities to prove myself and what I was all about and
I am thankful to people like that to this day.

I married and set up house at Gilmansleuch. A married shepherd
is different from a single shepherd. Part of the wage as a married
shepherd was a ton of potatoes per year, plus I had twelve sheep

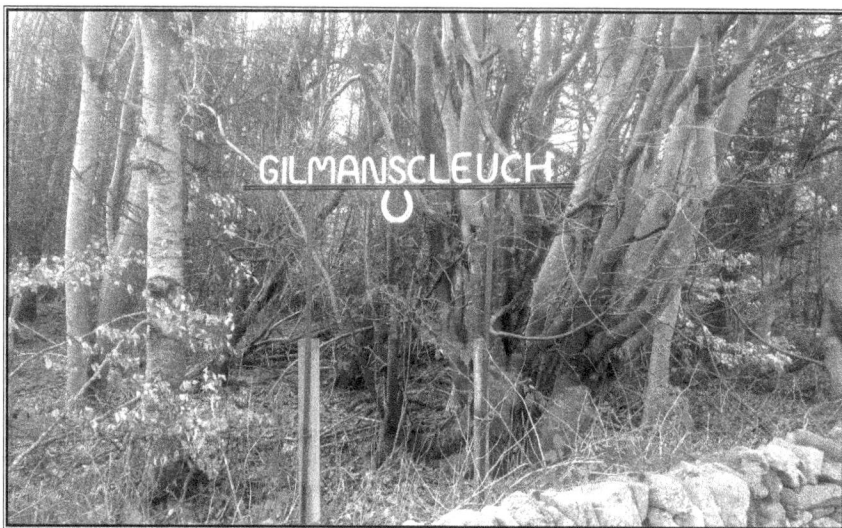

Farm sign for Gilmansleuch. *Photo by Frances Dickman.*

of my own. A lot of married shepherds had a cow and follower, which would be a cow that could raise a young calf or two. I never owned a cow, but I did get to keep young cattle and raise them up to sell, just a little bit extra on my wages and a way to save some money. A shepherd was more like an individual who took care of the livestock and in the process would put in extra hours at certain times earning part of the yearly bonuses. These bonuses would help out in different ways. The difference back home, compared to the United States, was the house came as part of the shepherd's wages; as with the potatoes and sheep, it was all just part of the wages earned.

The first registered Border Collie I ever owned was named Nell. She had two puppies; amazingly enough, they both turned out pretty nice. There was a female and a male that I kept. The male, a dog by the name of Glen, I really liked and the female was okay. I decided to sell her and so I advertised her. There was a man named Dave who came to see that female, but the reason he really came was because he'd heard about the male. After much negotiations trying to purchase the male, he finally offered me quite a bit of money and bought the two. It's kind of a funny story. I always remember when

**Jack at the house where he lived in Gilmansleuch before coming to the United States.** *Photo by Frances Dickman.*

Dave bought the dogs; I told him on the Glen dog, he could be a little tight on his outrun, but sometimes he'd be beautiful. I said if it was me, I'd leave him alone because I knew the nature of the dog. I knew if he put too much pressure on him, I had a feeling it would spoil him. I told him, "If you wait on this dog, it will all come right. If you push him, it might not."

A month later Dave had Glen entered in a trial I was going to. But by the time I got there, he had already run. Friends and many of the top handlers were giving me a hard time about Glen and why I had sold a dog with so much potential. Glen had shown himself well, in fact, to the point he was resold for three times more money. For me, that was the part I struggled to understand. It was hard for me as I felt I knew this dog very well and could not believe he had come that far in such a short time. As it turned out, the new owner took Glen home only to return him the next day. I never heard any more of Glen for a long time.

I was at a sheep sale one day when I ran into Dave, who had originally bought Glen from me. I asked him what happened to

**Part of the hill at Gilmansleuch where Jack shepherded for six years before coming to the United States.** *Photo by Frances Dickman.*

Glen? He kind of laughed and said, "You were right on that dog. I ended up selling Glen to Wales for sixty pounds and that dog never made it." I still believe, to this day, that Glen was a tremendous dog but was never given the chance. Again, this dog was a huge learning experience for me. It's not that I knew, I was just grasping at things in those days and following my mind about what to do with a dog here and there. It was this dog I thought so much of and yet he failed. I think the dog failed because of the pressure that was put on him. It opened up my mind that you can add pressure to a dog. You can be stubborn and add pressure to anything and want it your way, but it doesn't mean you are going to get it. That's exactly what happened to Glen. He just never made it because he didn't get the chance.

Looking back on the things like that from where I am now, it just goes more and more to prove how important the mind is. It's all about the mind. I can still see both of these dogs, and I can still see Glen.

I went to hundreds of trials and watched and enjoyed but never had the courage to go and run a dog. This changed after going to Gilmansleuch. I was at a show, which was one of the biggest agricultural shows in Scotland, The Kelso Show, which is still a very famous show. There were a bunch of us in the beer tent, young guys having fun and talking about the dogs. I guess we were telling each other we had the best dogs, when this guy came around and said, "Well, there is a trial at Salton. All you guys need to enter and then you can prove who has the best dog."

It ended up, one person entered and then another. That's really how I got into trialing. I don't know that I would ever have gone to compete in the trial if it hadn't been for that. I got entered in that trial, and from the day I entered I regretted it. I didn't feel I could do it. As the time approached, I got more and more scared. I always tell people, looking back at it, if it hadn't been for my dad and sister going with me to the trial, I would have never gone. I was sick to my stomach driving down the road that day and I wanted to turn back and go home. But I went and I ran Nan. I was one of the later ones to run and really had a good run. She made me proud and ran really well. I came off and there was quite a lot of people thinking I should have won it. I wasn't even in the top ten, which didn't really make a lot of difference. All that I was thinking was, it's passed; I just felt good that it went well.

And then Jock Richardson, owner of Wiston Cap, came over to me at the end of the trial and I'll never forget this. He put his hand on my shoulder and he said, "Never you mind, laddie; you'll be in the winner's circle someday." That meant more to me than ever winning a trial did. He was my idol. I thought he was tremendous, running his dogs; he had some gift. For me, personally, I loved to watch him run his dogs.

That was the start of a long career. It was during all this time at Gilmansleuch that I had lots of young dogs and would train them. In these times I used to train dogs and sell them again to make some extra cash. We were at a dog trial in Kelso, Scotland, at the Scottish National one year, and there were some Americans over: Ralph

Pulfer, Edgar Could, and George Conboy. I met them in the beer tent, and that's how I got to know them. They were looking to buy some dogs. They were going to come on a Sunday to see Bill and Nan, because I was thinking of selling them but they never showed up. My friend Tommy Wilson told me that Arthur Allen was coming over from the United States, and he would have him come over to look at my dogs. Little did I know at that time that through Arthur Allen coming to see these dogs would be how I was led to America. I can always remember the morning Arthur came to Gilmansleuch to see the two dogs. It was early morning; we had worked the dogs and came back up to the house. Authur was standing in the door to the house and he said, "You have a beautiful place to stay." I said, "yes, it's a pity I have to give it up next year." He never said anything, nor did he buy any dogs, he just left. I thought that was the end of the story and never thought much about it.

Two weeks later, I went to a trial at Westruther, which was a little local trial. And who was there but Arthur Allen. He came up to me and he said, "Remember, you were going to have to give up your position? There wouldn't be any chance you'd be interested in going to America?"

I said, "No, not in my wildest dreams." He went on and on about this and I said, " Look, you are wasting your time because I'm not even interested in going to America."

Arthur replied, "Well, Jack, I have a friend in America who wants a Scotsman to come over and work his dogs. He has a big ranch and this might be a great opportunity for you."

I told him, "Well, I really appreciate the chance but I have no intentions of leaving the country. I'm just not interested."

He finally said, "I've made a lot of inquiries about you, and you seem to be the ideal guy. If you don't mind, I'll take your name and address. You can negotiate with this guy and if you decide to go, fine. If you don't, there will be no bad feelings."

I said, "Well, that's fair enough."

Later, I got the call and we started negotiating. I got to the stage where I thought, if I don't do this, I am going to regret it the rest of my life. I decided to make the jump; we'd go across the water. It was a big decision in my life because I never had any intentions of doing this. Looking back, it's just like a dream, like a fairy tale to me. There are good parts and bad and there are always rich parts in a story and sad parts in a story.

It took about a year or maybe longer to get a working visa to come over. It was December of 1971 that we left Britain and made our way to the United States. I came and worked for a man by the name of Fred Bahnson from North Carolina. Fred was an ex state senator that owned a big farm just outside of Winston–Salem, in fact, he owned two places. He also had a dairy farm, and that's where I ventured to start my life in the United States. The one thing that he didn't want was me bringing my own dogs, so I tried to sell my dogs. It's funny looking back because both of these dogs I had, Bill and Nan, I was asking 100 pounds for, and I couldn't sell them. Today, I would hate to even try to put a value on them; it would be thousands of dollars. That's how much the dog world has changed since then. So, with me not being able to sell them, Fred agreed for me to be able to bring the dogs across the water with me.

I came over in December of 1971, and I shipped my two dogs a week before I was due to leave. Little did I know that when I arrived in America, one of my dogs would be stolen at the airport. I never was to see Nan again. That was sad in lots of ways, but sadder from the point that she was the one that started me on the way to all the success I found in my life. I have no idea to this day where Nan ever landed. I often think of her and wonder whether she would have changed my life or not, but that's just part of life. I was left with Bill when I got there. He was really the dog that built my reputation in America.

# Chapter 3:

# Off to America

Moving to America was a big step in my life. Everything was new. It was hard to leave my friends and family and move to a different country. Looking back on it, this was a tremendous experience. I was blessed by meeting the right people who, in turn, added to my success. The Bahnson family were the people who gave me the first opportunity and I will always owe a lot to them. I moved to North Carolina in 1971, moving onto the family farm 12 miles west of Winston-Salem, right as you cross the Yadkin River. The farm itself was beautiful, with gravel roads, man-made ponds, rolling hills and shade trees, more like a model type of place than a farm. When I first moved there, I moved into Senator Bahnson's summer residence. It was a beautiful log cabin overlooking one of the lakes. I stayed there for the first three months while a new mobile home was moved in and set up for the permanent residence. That is where I was to spend my next three years, trying years in some ways and great years in other ways.

When I first moved to North Carolina, the farm ran around 70 head of sheep and 30 or 40 head of cows on a thousand acres. Over the next three years, those numbers were increased to 700 head of sheep and around 200 head of cattle. We went from seven workers on the farm to cutting back to three plus myself because of the use of the border collies handing the livestock. I handled most of the livestock at that time on my own with the help of my dogs. We used to have a lot of trouble with pink eye in the cattle, while I was there. In the past, it would have taken three or four men to gather the pastures, take the cows in and doctor the pink eye. Because of the working border collies, this became a one-man job. I could usually just drive the jeep, cut out the cattle that had the pink eye, let the dog bring them into the barn, doctor them, and then let them out. Border Collies are a work tool, they are a play tool, they are a bit of everything; in my opinion, in many ways, these dogs are greatly underrated.

Mr. Bahnson was more interested in the breeding side of the dogs when I arrived. He had bought many good dogs and part of my job was to train his dogs and run them at trials. My first trial in America was in Delaware in June of 1972. I took four dogs, three of Mr. Bahnson's and one of my own. I ended up in the qualifying, placing first, second, third, and fifth; then second and fourth in the finals. I was off to a really good start. The dog that was second in the finals was my Bill dog.

The next trial I went to was the Bluegrass in Kentucky. This was my second trial in America and again I ran the four dogs. They were all in the placing once again. At this trial, I met a man from Wisconsin by the name of Larry Reif, who was in the area and sightseeing. He was accompanied by his daughter and, to me, was a complete stranger. He owned a Border Collie and was interested in talking to me about the dogs. Unknown to me, Larry Reif was another man that was to play an important role in my life.

On the farm in Wisconsin where Jack had the opportunity to form his first partnership with Larry Reif, on the left.

I returned back from that trial and about two weeks later got a bunch of pictures in the mail that Larry had taken of me and my dogs. I wrote and thanked him and we became very good friends. Later on, I ended up selling him a dog, and our friendship grew from that.

Just after I first came over to the USA, my boss, Fred Bahnson, had two litters of puppies. Both litters were very well bred, nice pups, well marked. One of the litters had a male pup which for some reason I was drawn to. This pup was a bit unusual because of his tail. I understand that lots of puppies carry their tails up, but this one was more like a little pig. It was really curled, and my boss, Fred, would always bother me about why I liked a pup with a tail carriage like that.

One day he came by the house and in our conversation said, "I know you like the pup with the tail like a pig. Here is what I want to do. I am going to give him to you. I want to keep one from the other litter as well but you have to promise to give both the same chance."

So the "little pig" pup became mine. I named him Glen; he was a double bred Wiston Cap. Fred's pup was a Wiston Cap son, from a female out of Tom Watson's Craig, his name, Mirk. As the pups grew up, they were both nice dogs, good natured, with Mirk, maybe the nicer of the two. By seven months old Mirk was doing well and showing lots of promise, whereas Glen had no interest in stock whatsoever.

The reason I write this story is just another notch of experience in my training, which I was about to gain from my dog. Time went on and Glen stayed the same, and at one point friends came to visit and saw Glen. They immediately tried to buy him, and I asked, "Why would you want a dog like that? He has no desire, although well mannered, with a good nature."

"Well," he said, "I like his looks."

He was a big, well built, dog, the tail was a lot better, but still not right to suit my interest but he was determined to have him. I struggled to understand why, and he said, "I want him for a stud dog."

I guess that was it. I said, "No, I'm going to keep him," but I said if ever I should chang my mind I would get in touch. Well, time went on, Glen stayed much the same, so I called my friend, maybe around October and said I may part with him. He said it might be the end of the year before he could get back to pick him up, which I said was fine.

About two or three weeks later, I was working on sheep in the pens and just happened to notice Glen watching, even showing a little eye. So I slipped up to the gate and released a few sheep.

Glen immediately flanked around, so I kept moving the sheep as his instinct kept growing. From here on, Glen never looked back.

This was a dog that went with me everyday, was exposed to livestock all the time, and had never ever showed any sign of interest. Yes, he was well behaved, knew how to listen and knew above all how to accept a correction. Within the next month I had Glen pretty well broke and could do all my work with him, cattle or sheep. He was very powerful yet had great contact with an ease and stillness on how to use it.

In November, my friend called to inquire about Glen. I said, "You will not believe it, I was ready to give you this dog, but I doubt very much if now you could buy him today." He decided to come see Glen, but in the end Glen stayed with me.

This was December, and the Blue Grass Trial in Lexington, Kentucky, was to be in early June. I decided to enter Glen, so this was his first competition. I will always remember: he had a good outrun, would not stop at the top, and split the sheep, coming down with two while leaving one behind. I finally did get him stopped and sent him back for the single, which he fetched in the manner he should have brought the three in the first place. The following year Glen and I went back to Kentucky and took the blue ribbon. He was a great dog, maybe one of the better I have ever had. But above all he taught me more than most people could.

The following year a World Championship was held in Delaware. I took Dryden Craig and Glen to compete and remember saying when I left home, "If I do well at all, it will be with Glen." It was a long two-day drive, and I arrived the evening before the trial. There was a group of handlers going out to the university farm to give their dogs a run. They asked me to go and, although reluctant, I went along.

The pasture where they were working had a barn in the bottom corner that the sheep wanted to make their safety zone. Like a fool, I took Glen out and blocked sheep, helping the other handlers have

Jack in the midst of a demonstration in Wisconsin with three patient dogs waiting as Bill does his work. Photo from the late 70s or early 80s.

a chance to run their dogs. Little did I know at that time what the outcome was for myself and Glen. At the trial the following day came, I walked to the post and sent Glen. He had a good outrun, lift, and fetch; everything felt good. We started up the drive and about halfway up Glen stopped, looked at me, left his sheep and returned to my feet. So that was it, I walked off, puzzled and disappointed.

Not only was I to be disappointed in this trial but it turned out that was to be Glen's final trial. I still puzzle today over what really happened but, whatever it was, I could never get Glen's drive right again. It was the last thing that I would have thought about because I had all the confidence in the world in that dog. Glen, in himself, was a great dog and even though this part went missing, he will forever be thought of as something special. Thanks Glen, a lesson learned. It's better to look for the help your dog needs, than to show off what your dog can do.

Three years went by in North Carolina, and I was getting to the stage where I just wasn't happy, so I talked to my boss at that time. I said to him, "You know, you've been so good to me, the last

Once the sheep are in the open pen, Glen, acting as a gate, is in full control with his partners awaiting.

thing I want to do is for us to fall out or have bad feelings. Yet, I think the time has come when you and I need to think about parting company."

To cut a long story short, that's what happened; I decided to leave. At that point, I didn't know what I was going to do. I was thinking of going back to Britain. During this time, Larry Reif, who had become a really good friend, was looking for a job up in the Wisconsin/Minnesota area while I was looking in different parts of the country. About that time, I was actually hired to go out to Oregon to work for a farm that used to run a flock of Hampshire sheep. The job would have included taking a string of sheep on the show circuit. When all of the sudden, I got a letter from Larry in Wisconsin wondering if I'd ever be interest in starting on my own. I called him up and I said, "It was just a dream, there's no way." But he said to me, "There is a way. I want you to fly to Wisconsin—I want to talk to you." I ended up flying up there and he offered me a partnership on his farm. So that's what I did; I went up there and entered into a partnership in Wisconsin.

My family moved to Wisconsin, lived in a trailer on the farm for about a year and a half. The partnership was struggling for income so we talked. At this time Larry offered me a lease on the farm if I would stay. And that's what I did. After getting the lease, I made a trip to Scotland and bought eight dogs, which started my kennel. I couldn't afford to buy what I wanted, but I bought the best I could. Since that time, I kept upgrading the dogs to improve the standard of the kennel. To this day, that's still my philosophy. I'm always looking for a better dog than I've got, not to win a trial as much as to build the kennel up. Once I got the kennel running, I started hitting the trial circuit and going to lots of trials. Through the late 70s and early 80s I was pretty successful; I had my share of wins and began building up my reputation. Of course, when you get a good reputation, everything starts to work.

# Chapter 4:

# *Shepherding and Trialing in America*

During my time in Wisconsin, my goals took new directions as I began to judge trials, and this led me into the world of teaching clinics. I was fortunate enough to run in many trials, from the south to the north of the United States and up into Canada. I won the Canadian Open and the American Grand Finals to name a few of my trialing successes.

I remember it was 1973 when they had the world trials in Delaware. I went out to compete with my dog Bill, who came to the United States with me from Scotland. The other dog I ran was a dog that really belonged to Arthur Allen. At the World Trials I ended up doing well. I won the American Championship which qualified Bill to run in the World Trials where I ended up fourth. In 1976, they had another World Trial in Delaware. I went out to compete with Craig and ended up second. That was quite an experience.

During my time in Wisconsin, I kept buying and importing dogs and getting dogs for other people. I was going back and forth to Britain. I ended up buying a dog by the name of Dryden Craig from a great friend of mine, Tommy Wilson. Tommy and I spent many great times in Scotland before we left, and we've spent many great times in America since.

I remember being home one year, and he had a dog named Dryden Craig; he was a nice dog. He was a son of Wiston Cap and his mother was a daughter of Gilchrist's Spot. When I saw Tommy run Craig, I really liked him. I can always remember Tommy coming and telling me he had gotten and offer on the dog and asking me, "what would you do if he was your dog?"

I said, "Do you want to win or do you want to make money?"

He said, "I want to win."

I told him I would keep that one so Tommy ended up keeping him. I told him at the time, "You know, I'll never be able to afford to buy Dryden Craig, but if you don't get along with him in the next year and decide to sell him, I'll try to help you."

So that's what happened. Tommy decided to sell him and he wrote me a letter. He was going to sell Dryden Craig and also a female. I wrote back to him and told him I would buy the female and I would try to find a buyer for Dryden Craig. By the time he got my letter, he had sold the female. I called him up and said, "If you still have Dryden Craig, I'll buy him." I bought Craig in March, took him to the World Trials in June, and ended up the Reserve Champion.

Dryden Craig was to be the backbone of my kennel over the years. He was a great dog; strong, very powerful, maybe too powerful for the normal trial field. I always knew Craig would give me 100 percent. He was a tough dog to run and he was hard to run; it was just eagerness rather than bull-headedness. He was such a keen-going dog. I would love to have another like him. He was a good looking dog, bold and to this day, I still have lines going back to Dryden Craig.

**At the North American Championship with Dryden Craig and Buff.**

I have purchased many great dogs that came across the water. One dog I bought was named Jed; again, Tommy came into the picture. When I bought Jed, Tommy and I saw her at this trial and a man named Alec Waugh owned her. I can't remember if it was the Scottish National or not but I said to Tom, "I like that dog." He encouraged me to go and ask Alec if he would sell Jed; I didn't really think he would. I went and inquired and the answer was yes. So I asked if he would mind if I could come and see her at his place. I remember going to Alec's farm and seeing him working Jed on the big flock. She was really good and I bought her. She was the dog that went on to win two American Championships for me. Jed was a tremendous female, the complete opposite from Dryden Craig. Where Dryden Craig was tough and pushy, Jed was stylish, classy, and easy to handle. She was a female with class, balance and tremendous feel. Jed was a dog that lacked a little power, but we managed to put it all together, and in the end, she turned out to be a top dog in my kennel. Although she was a great trial dog and maybe won more money than any dog I ever ran, she was not a top breeder.

I also bought a dog through another good friend of mine, Jonny Wilson. He was a good friend and a great asset to me. I bought a dog through Johnny named Jan. Jan was owned by Bill Elliot who ran her at the Scottish National. I believed Bill had quite a good run, but he failed to make all his gates. Upon Jan's failing to make her gates, Bill was a little disappointed. Johnny talked to Bill after the run and asked if she might be for sale. Bills' reply was "ask me tomorrow."

So the next day the purchase was made and Jan ended up in my kennel. Jan was out of Baxter's Betty by Baxter's Craig. Jan was another dog that was to be a huge asset in my kennel. I eventually bred Jan to Dryden Craig and those puppies were something else; the cross just clicked. Many, many great dogs came out of Jan and Craig.

# Chapter 5:

# Turkey and Hog Stories

Through the years, I have had many unique experiences. Things that again have been added towards my knowledge and know-how and have given me the chance to look at dogs from many different angles. We all often think of the trial field, and who and what we can learn from it, but much of my learning has come from other sources. Everyday life, people, my friends—there is so much to be learned if we study how we live and what we do, especially how we handle ourselves. Studying people and thinking about how they come up with the answers they do has given me many answers to solving problems and finding easier ways when it comes to training my dogs. I have had the chance to work and be challenged by many different types of situations that have added to my experience and understanding of what the dog is all about, and what they can teach us, if only we will look and accept.

**Glen, Bill, and Dryden Craig from left to right, show the geese who's the master.**

Years ago, I was asked by a large turkey operation in Minnesota if I would be willing to come and show what the Border Collie would be able to accomplish for them in their multi-million dollar turkey operation. Though I had worked a few chickens or geese with them in the past, I accepted, but really had little or no idea what I was walking into. It was a night job where we were to load two semi loads of turkeys. I can remember walking into the turkey barn with my dog. It seemed like there were a million birds in there. Seeing the dog made them panic, but after some time they settled down. My job was to keep the birds moved up to the elevators that were to convey the turkeys up and onto the truck, while others were filling them into cages ready for shipping. As the night went on, the work got easier as I studied and watched the reaction of the birds. We loaded two trucks, I sold two dogs, and another experience was under my belt.

Another experience for me was working and loading pigs. On a nice spring day, a car drove in the driveway as I headed to the house for lunch. The driver got out and asked if I was the man with the Border Collies. Of course I said yes, and he asked if he could see them work. I had two dogs tied up at the house so I went, got them, jumped the fence, and worked my dogs on sheep in the field across the road. When I finished, he asked, "How much do you want for them."

I said, "They are not for sale, these are my trial dogs."

The gentleman's name was George Wood, and unknown to me at that time, he was a friend of my boss. George was pretty persistent on buying my two dogs, so I asked what he wanted them for. He said, "I run a one hundred thousand hog operation near Elizabeth City, North Carolina and I want to use these dogs to see if they can help out in the everyday operation."

My answer was, "These dogs have never seen a pig, far less worked one," so I said my answer was, "No."

Although George was determined to buy, I was just as determined not to sell. We went down to the barn where he bought two pups, under the condition we keep them three months at which time we would bring the two pups plus two trained dogs to Elizabeth City and try to work them on the pigs.

When we arrived, the operation was simple, but at the same time huge. He would purchase two semi truckloads of hogs every morning, seven days a week, and sell two loads of finished hogs the same day. The idea was to use the dogs to load the hogs. The operation was set up like a fairly large racetrack. All the way around the outside were three or four-acre lots, which were all numbered one to 500. Each lot of four acres was roughly half open, the rest in brush and small trees. The idea for the brush was for shade. Each lot fed into the racetrack as a means of moving the hogs from the lot to the loading dock. As we went out that morning, the heat of the day was increasing.

George said, "Jack, I want you to go into lot 235, there should be 253 hogs; with the help of your dogs I would like to see you try and bring the hogs onto the track, up to the loading dock, and if you are successful you might sell two dogs."

A perfect example of eye power and control of the Border Collie as Glen showes the hog who's in control.

Being a little leery, I said to George, "Wait a minute, you understand these dogs have never seen a pig, far less worked them."

His reply was, "Don't worry, I have plenty men who will come help if needed."

I can remember that day I had on a pair of light colored trousers and a light colored shirt. I was getting hot and sweaty as I made my way into the lot. By this time, the hogs lay comfortably asleep in the shade. I crawled in and tried to wake them but all I got was a grunt. As I found my way, at times crawling on my hands and knees to the far side, I began encouraging my dogs to bite or nip a little at the pigs. It did not take too long for the pigs to realize that these dogs meant business and with some grunts and some squeals the pigs began to give. It may have taken 15 or 20 minutes to get these hogs on the move and out the gate onto the track.

On command Glen singles this pig out, a good shed with the dog in control.

I will always remember George coming up, putting his hand on my shoulder and saying, "Jack, I have seen thousands and thousands of pigs come out of these lots, but that's the first time I have ever seen one emptied." He continued, "usually they would get them near the gate, the pigs would break with a handful escaping, and because of the heat they would have to let them go."

We loaded 500 pigs that morning with my light pants and shirt a little different color.

As we finished, George said, "I know you're hot, tired, and your dogs are to about give out, but in lot 373 among the 250 or so hogs in that lot are about seven or eight that are about double the size of the others because they know how to escape the loading procedure." He asked if I would be willing to try to get them out so they could be loaded on the semi. Of course, that was a challenge to me. I made several tries with my dogs to get the larger pigs separated, but each time the pigs would break back and remix, so the procedure was repeated. Finally, after four or five attempts, we succeeded with two dogs and seven pigs on their way to the loading chute. We cleaned up after loading the pigs and moved on to the house where we were served a first class lunch. While we ate lunch, George had a pad of paper, bombarding me with questions on how to work these dogs. After a lengthy discussion he bought two dogs and we left for our return journey back home.

I can remember saying to Mr. Bahnson, "After answering all the questions, I do not think they have any idea and was sure the dogs would be returning to Win-Mock-Farm."

However, after they made one or two trips to Win-Mock and got some help with handling their dogs, they seemed pretty satisfied. It must have been three months or so later, Mr. Bahnson was returning to the area to go duck hunting. I asked if he would mind going by George's office and find out how the two dogs had turned out. Upon his return, Fred Bahnson said when he saw George his first question was, "Jack wants to know about the dogs?"

Fred said, "Yes he does; he is always wanting to make sure the customer is satisfied."

"Well," said George, "when you go back tell Jack when he sold me the two dogs, I thought he had robbed me, but tell him today he could not buy them back for twice the money."

He said, "Normally seven days a week it took six men to empty lots and load hogs. Now one man and two dogs can do the same operation with less stress and way easier than it had ever been done."

This became another adventure, a true story, a happy customer, and these dogs showing off their ability, purpose, and what they are all about, provided they are given the chance.

# Chapter 6:

# Jack's Take on Clinics

It was back in the late 70s when I was first approached to do my first clinic. I had been asked to go judge a trial by the vet students in Auburn, Alabama. They were short on finances, so they approached me to put on a training clinic to help offset the expenses of the trial. I had heard about clinics but had never seen one or knew much about them. Little did I know at that time how this was going to change my life.

After being asked several times I finally gave in and said I would try but, in all honesty, it was not with an open mind. In fact, it was a mind filled with fear, with little or no real confidence. As time for the clinic grew closer, the answers and feelings inside me became more insecure. I will never forget the night before that first clinic. I was scared and wanted to hide, anything but go out there the next morning and face all the folks who had registered to try to get help with their dogs.

Looking back now at how I felt makes me believe in what it must be like for our dogs. Fear is a delicate emotion; it can help but it can also hurt. It can build your confidence or it can take away from it—even destroy it. This is something, again, I think about when it comes to training dogs.

When fear enters a dog's mind, it makes for a delicate situation; much the same as fear inside ourselves. The clinic drew participants from over ten states. One was a lady from Virginia, Ethel Conrad. Ethel was to become a very dear friend. She was the founder of seminars and clinics, the one who pushed, promoted, and was a leading figure in building our Border Collie world into what it has become today. It was three weeks after the clinic when Ethel called and asked if I would go to Virginia and put a clinic on at her home at White Post, Virginia. This started a long relationship between us; over the years I must have put on over fifty clinics for Miss Ethel.

For those who knew Ethel, she was this wonderful lady until you met the other side. Sometimes it was Ethel's way or no way, and when she had something to say, you had better be prepared to listen because you can bet you were going to hear it. Ethel and I had many ups and downs in our time but we thought so much of each other, there was never a doubt in our friendship. She was a tremendous lady; one who touched many lives and did much for all whom she touched.

Clinics kept taking me on the road meeting many remarkable people as well as taking me to new parts of the USA and Canada. It would be hard for me to put into words half of everything the clinics have taught me, far less express the experience from all the places I visited which have added so much value to my life.

Yes, clinics are for teaching others—and it's hard for me to explain what I feel there is in a clinic for participants to gain. People come to a clinic with the idea they know what they want; they know there are problems and they want them answered, which is fair enough. From my point of view, I will try to help them as much as I

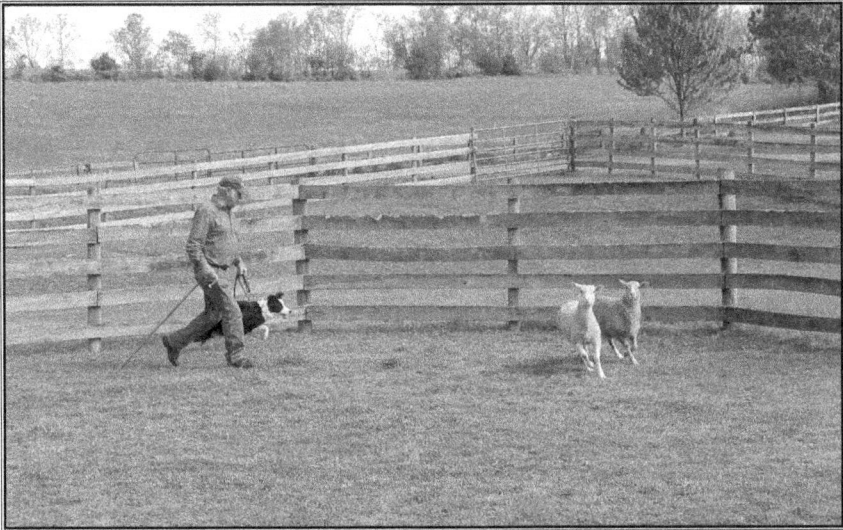

Jack is giving a dog the freedom to be wrong while observing how the dogs finds and feels the pressure point to handle the sheep. With assistance from Jack the dog should begin to open up. *Photo by Tom Moates.*

know how. To be honest, the person who comes with an open mind, hoping he or she will take away training ideas, will possibly leave with much more information than those who don't. They will be able to try out many of the answers they witnessed as they watched and listened to the clinician. Why? Because they come with an open mind and that mind will convey to them the answers they need.

Not only will it convey, but it will plant the seed to grow. It is no different than what I say about dogs; the open mind is the one who learns the easy way and never forgets. As I think of the number of clinics I have given, the answer to that "open mind" comes to my mind. I never plan or ever think about a clinic ahead of time. Many times after the first day, I will think about a dog or a person, and I will evaluate the progress and what needs to be changed to come up with the answers. Most of the time I find the dog comes up with the answer that in turn answers the question I have been asking myself. The dog comes up with the answers because it's given time to think. It's the small corrections to an open mind that gives the best results. Too many people want positive answers, and yet if we asked ourselves "is it that easy to get the positive or everything right all the time?" the answer is no. Perfection is something I strive for but, for me, will never be achieved.

When I look back on my clinic experiences today, the answers I have been given are profound. When people study their dogs, answers usually come easy. When we make a dog follow our minds, the dog cannot give us answers.

Today, putting on clinics comes so much easier simply because I let the dog give the answer. If the dog is wrong, I correct it by making the wrong harder and in turn the right becomes easy. This takes away the fight between dog and handler allowing both the dog and handler to achieve their goal. It amazes me even today how easy it has become compared to how hard it used to be. Helping dogs find the answers to their wrongs gives positive reaction while trying to make a dog right is questionable. The clinic circuit has not only been a success in my small sheepdog world, but its been an education which, in my mind, would have been impossible to reach otherwise. So a big thanks to my students, participants, and the people involved who have supported me all these years.

# Chapter 7:

# *Jaws*

After several clinics at Ethel's in White Post, Virginia, I met a student named Frank Moffat. Frank was a very good friend of Ethel's and was to become a very good friend of mine. He shared the accommodations in the school house with me during the clinics—the school house was a one-room house on Ethel's property that was to become my home on my visits to Ethel's farm.

It was the Thursday night before the start of a three-day clinic. Likely as not, we would have had a few cocktails after dinner. Frank and I were in the process of getting ready for bed, when all of a sudden Frank says, "You know Jack, you're always joking or playing pranks on us, so I thought at this clinic I would play one on you, but I am thinking of changing my mind."

"Why's that?" I asked Frank, and then his story flowed out.

"Well I've got this dog, who I've nick-named 'Jaws,'" he said.

"All the dog wants to do is kill a sheep."

I said, "He can't be that bad."

Frank's reply was, "I'm telling you, he will grab the sheep, pull it to the ground, and try to worry it."

I said, "Then what do you think you are going to do with him?"

The answer was to put him to sleep. After a little bit of conversation about Jaws, yes, possibly a wee argument, I said to Frank, "Tell you what to do, Frank, just bring Jaws to the clinic as planned and we'll take it from there."

The next morning arrived and the clinic got underway. I had worked six or seven dogs before it came to Jaws's turn. In the meantime, Frank had Jaws down at the ring watching and observing the clinic. The ring is where I like to start young dogs, or take dogs further along in training, back to help solve their problems. I feel it makes it easier for me and much easier for the dog. Frank had Jaws on a five or six foot chain. He had part of the chain wrapped around his arm and Jaws, as expected, was a little hyper. He was driving himself crazy as he watched the movement and other dogs work.

At my clinics, first go round, I always have people introduce themselves and their dog, give a little history about the dog, the stage where he is, and the problems they are having. So Frank enters the ring, introduces himself and Jaws, and tells the story.

" Well, Jaws is a little aggressive," Frank began.

"No, Frank," I piped in, "that's not what you told me last night. You said, Jaws is a killer, all he wants to do is kill."

Frank went back to his introduction, and again, I interrupted and said, "So what is the future for Jaws?"

Frank replied, "I am going to take him home and have him put down."

At this time, I told Frank to go ahead and proceed as he would have at home. As I watched, I saw a frantic dog, doing much as Frank had said the dog would do. Remember, this dog was still on the leash with most of the chain wrapped around Frank's arm, with

Frank keeping a firm hold. If Jaws reached the sheep, he would grab hold, pull one to the ground, and the only way to get him to let go was to pop him on the head until he would release.

I watched for two or three minutes, then said, "Give him to me."

So I took Jaws and much the same thing happened. I tried everything I knew and after a few minutes was going to quit, when all of a sudden Jaws made a dive at the sheep. I gave a firm and positive ah..hh, and Jaws gave, not much, but gave. I was lucky enough to see that give, a small change in the body movement, an ease up of his desperate eye.

Instantly I reached down, caught the collar and chain and released Jaws. I threw the chain out of the ring with the comment, " I don't need it." Don't get me wrong; it was far from over, as Jaws continued on his "catch to kill" motions. I continued doing the best I could to correct him and within five minutes at the most, I stopped and said, "I've got him now." To some at this stage, they may see little or no change. For me, I saw a clear, open change in the proceedings and a new method being born before my eyes. The afternoon turn for Jaws arrived, and again I took over. The battle began and a little light started to show again: after about five minutes we quit.

The relationship between Jaws and myself was changing, a feeling that's hard to explain. Saturday morning, Jaws and my journey continued with gains and losses to each other shared. That afternoon, with Jaws and my big breakthrough getting better, he got another five minute turn. As we ended, I said to the participants at the clinic, "We'll work this dog outside tomorrow."

For me, no thoughts of Jaws entered my mind until his turn to work came up. Before our session started, I explained to the participants that I knew little better than they what the result might be until things happened. The only difference was, Jaws had given me something. I don't know what, but I could feel it. It was like "trust me Jack, I trust you."

Our session outside started rough but answers came and within our five minutes there were huge changes. On his afternoon turn, I was sending Jaws 100 yards or more, stopping him, and calling him off. The answer to Jaws and our problems were over. I was a happy man, had a happy friend, and a changed dog. Jaws went on to be a great dog for Frank. Not only was Jaws a great work dog, he was successful in trials, and was in Frank's words, "a dog with power, balance, and feel." A dog who, for my friend, gave it all and made a friendship stronger. There were no longer thoughts of the dog leaving this world but more the opposite, a future bloomed with large opportunities, all there to be gained.

The story of Jaws continued, not only had he changed, but in the process, unknown to Jaws and myself, he had given me a change in my training method. It was a change I studied and felt, and maybe most of all opened up my mind to a new method, which even today is still growing. The events recounted in this story not only changed my training methods, but changed my thoughts in life. The same applies to ourselves as applies to the dog. It's the freedom to be wrong, provided we are willing to correct, and as we correct, we give freedom to think. It's really the freedom behind the correction and how we read it and handle it that counts. We are so guilty of giving praise that the second a right appears, we never leave time to see or study the reaction. This is what the Jaws episode taught me most: that making a mind does not come close to using it. Few will ever know what Jaws gave me, but myself, I am still amazed. I think often of our venture and come up with one answer; it was meant to be.

# Chapter 8:

# *Who Am I?*

To sum, "Who am I?" I have loved sheep, livestock, and dogs from as far back as I can remember. It was my dream come true, at age 16, when I got my first job as a shepherd. I think if I had been asked then, I would have worked for nothing. These early years are a memory I will never forget. Who would have known then where it was to take me, change me, and give me an education, better than anyone could have taught.

The trial side was something I always enjoyed, but, in the beginning, I never even thought I'd go and compete. It was something I was talked into; otherwise I doubt if I would have ever been brave enough to try it. I am not one who ever thinks I am good enough. I always remember my dear friend the late John Wilson telling me, "You know your problem, Knox, is you never believe in yourself, yet you are as good as anyone who goes to the post." Many times I have

Jack and Jim at Soldier Hollow the year they won the trial. Jack says of this dog, "Jim is at the ready. So many dogs are very mechanical when they work. You can see here Jim is in contact with the sheep as he waits for the command to come in." *Photo by Anita Pratt.*

thought of these words and known deep down how right he was. But then looking back, that is who I am and who I want to be. There are many things about who I am, if changed, might help but it's not about being the best that counts, it's about being me. I have lived a life of happiness with my dogs—a life where my dogs have guided me through ups and downs and given me insight into my future.

Writing this book came about by many different requests, for lots of different reasons. The main link for me came at the end of a two day clinic held here at home. I was approached by a very dear friend who, over the years, had taken in many of my clinics, and she said, "I know you have had two long days and you are more than ready to get done, but if possible, I would like to talk to you for a few minutes at the end." I don't know if the words are exact, but she said something like this, "Jack, we have talked to your wife, Kathy, and asked her if she felt it would be okay to ask you if there was any way we could talk you into writing a book." Before I could answer, she continued, "There are many of us who have been talking and are amazed at how you keep coming up with the answers on why our dogs act the way they do; within minutes you tell and show us change. We know that you are not going to be around forever, yet feel you have so much more to give. We have watched and seen amazing work turn into, what seems to us, magic. We know, for us, there is not near enough time left to gain what you have to offer. So, please, would you do this for us?"

My first reaction was, "So you are telling me I am going to die?" But in all fairness, this is what got me thinking of how I could give back to the people who made it all possible. Who I am will play a big role in many of the chapters I will write in this book. Sometimes I get amazed at my life: my beliefs, ambitions, rights and wrongs, praise, corrections, successes, failures, wins, and losses. I am different from most and for some, may even seem a bit odd. But it's me, who I am, and why I am happy with the way I am. Some may ask, "What does this have to do with dogs or training?" This is my training.

These dogs have trained me, or should I say, opened up my understanding of life, the rights, the wrongs, the good, and the bad. It's the people who have reached out for help who are the ones that have guided me to many of the answers I have found. The problem is, most don't look for them. Sometimes, when we feel we know it all, we miss the biggest share. I will try to break down some of the words when, if we think of them, make so much sense.

Today, it's all about winning, so let's start with a win versus a loss. For me, there is nothing wrong with a win, provided we get it the correct way, that being, to train your dog to the best of its ability and leave others to do the same. It's not done that way. We train to win any way we can even though most times we know it's wrong and as a result, end up less than honest with each other. When things go wrong, instead of taking the blame, we pass that on to everything else: the judge, the sheep, the set out, the list goes on and on. For me, it's pretty simple, if we correct ourselves, the quality of work will get better. The enjoyment of trialing will grow and, above all, our dogs will get the chance they deserve.

Pride in our work is, to me, something that is disappearing. Pride is another word, when thought of correctly, that can have a huge impact on our sport. We have to remember, if we want our dogs' breeding to improve, we have to let our dogs show their strengths or weaknesses. When we hide the wrong, it does not make a right. If we correct the wrong, the answer is possible. A loss is something none of us want, but in saying that, it's what 99 percent of us get as there is only one winner. Many things can be gained out of a loss, the biggest being how to accept the loss. I always tell people, it's easy to accept a win, but much harder to take a loss. If taken the correct way, a loss can be a start on how to get better. A good loser works at keeping an open mind, which if used correctly, comes up with answers. If you only accept your loss by making up excuses, then there is nothing to be gained.

Growing up, as a kid, if I did not accept a loss, I would be told that, if I could not accept the result, I should not be allowed to play. This is a far cry from today when we are praised for a poor try. Ambition can mean many things, but, for me, it is trying to be better. I don't need to go win the trial, I just need to try; but there is no way I want to try without knowing I have a chance. I do not want to be there if I know myself or my dogs are not capable.

On praise, it's one I'm not too big on. Oh, like most, we all like it, but usually when we do well, we know it. Although praise is nice, it's not really necessary. For me, my ambition is to have the chance to go out there and compete. But I must feel I have a dog and myself worthy of that chance. I get as much or more out of watching and listening as I do running my dog. I was once told by one I looked up to and admired, "You will learn more by watching the best rather than by trying to be the best." Success to me sure feels good, but failure is where I learn the most. When I am successful, of course I feel good, maybe too much so. While gloating in my success, I might forget how I got there. Failure, on the other hand, is disappointment that makes me think more about why I failed. This of course leads to correcting where I went wrong and, if corrected the right way, should be a step towards succeeding. For me, to see someone working on making the way from the bottom up is success and, in a way, possibly the biggest winner.

Anger is another word which, when thought of the right way, can give so many answers. I can honestly say, there are few times in my life when I felt angry that it has helped. It may have made me feel better at the time, but when I look back on it, my regrets outweigh my gains. Again, the dogs have taught me that being mad does not give them answers. It adds fear, confusion, and closes the mind when we should be opening it up. When we get mad, we force our answers, making our dogs follow our minds because of fear, threat, or force. We get our answers but I doubt the dog gets anything except "I better do as I am told." For me, not only does this take away from our dog on why, but also puts doubts there, which will haunt us as we progress with our dog's training.

It is no different from ourselves, when someone is angry at us, we either retaliate with anger or shy back from fear. When really, if we both gave, we both would win and end up happy because we freed our minds, which when freed, brings relief. Don't get me wrong, like anyone else, I still get angry. These dogs have taught me, or should I say, are teaching me, how to handle my anger. It amazes me when I think of the times when I have been angry, frustrated, and the amount of pressure I have put on dogs to try to come up with answers. Now I work on the complete opposite, taking pressure off, leaving openings for a wrong so I can correct it, leaving my dog the chance to give his or her answer.

All, or at least 70% of what I write here has been taught to me by my dogs or your dogs. Study their wrongs and they will show you how to help them come right the easy way. When two minds come together it makes things easy, a far cry from the one mind who wants to fight the other, or fear the other.

I would like to focus on the word "respect." This is something that means so much to me in my training and in my life. It seems we make so many excuses when it comes to what respect means. When used right, respect can give both ourselves and our dogs the clear and easy answers. Many times we give praise without really meaning it. Other times we criticize each other without having a reason or, maybe, just to make us feel important. I hear people make fun of others in ways that, to me, makes them much less of a person. It is the same with our dogs; we blame the dog many times when really it's ourselves to blame. If we respect each other, we would not give false praise. I doubt we would criticize without reason and certainly would not be making fun of people we respect.

On our dogs, hopefully we would, through respect, think more and in doing so allow our dogs the chance to think. In the process this would give us answers without us adding pressure to the dog, who was actually right in the first place.

In clinics I give now, the first thing I look for in your dog is respect. If respect is missing, most of the time the first question I ask myself is, "What caused this? Does the dog not understand?" Definitely, this is the first answer I will go out to seek. To gain respect, one has to give so that the other has the same chance. How do we get a dog to give who possibly does not know how? We start by correction—how much depends on the dog and how long it has been allowed to disrespect. The correction gets the dog to give, to think, but the answer comes from the freedom behind it. There is a fine line between "respect" and "make," and it all comes together on allowing the dog the chance. One may have a few failures, but patience and time allow great results.

I can give many examples of dogs who changed in the matter of five minutes, but a good example is a dog I had in a recent clinic. This dog had been to two or three different trainers, and I was told

Jack and Coach, his main dog, getting ready to demonstrate at a clinic in Lexington, Virginia. *Photo by Tom Moates.*

by its owner, "As long as you kept it under control you were fine. The minute you tried to give it freedom, you lost control and it was all over."

The first time we tried to work this dog, we were in lots of trouble and recovering from what I would call a wreck. I stated that this dog had lots of problems, maybe more than I know how to handle. I explained on the second turn we would work this dog in the ring or small area where I like to start young dogs and take it from there. He was the last dog I had to work that night, and I said to leave him on-leash and give the dog to me.

We started out pretty crazy, but after a minute or so I could see and feel small answers developing. I continued about five minutes total before stopping, then explained some of the small changes I could see and feel in this dog. In the five minutes we worked, the dog was never off-leash. But I could feel his tension giving, the hyperness leaving, and the mind relaxing. For me, it was a good place to stop.

"In all fairness," I said, "I still am pretty insecure in my own mind about the dog's future."

The following morning we worked this dog first thing as the owner had to catch a ferry. As we gathered around the ring, I asked if anyone had a long line and ended up with two pieces of rope tied together. I explained this rope is not to be used to try to make the dog right, rather to hold the pressure if he went wrong, hopefully allowing him the chance to think should he start losing his mind, or in other words, "blow up."

We started out and right away I could feel change. As he gave, I gave, the rope was dropped, and the answers became apparent; I would give freedom, he would give respect. I could walk away, call him off, and send him. The dog was, for me, completely changed. The answer was the respect we gained for each other in the five minutes we worked the previous night.

I think one of the biggest mistakes we make is, when we get improvement, we want more. For me, the smaller the change the bigger the answer, provided we wait. It's funny when we finished with this dog the first night, after just five minutes, I could feel that people wanted more. I knew deep down this dog had given all he had to give and more. My belief is, when they give you a little and you accept, this is their reward. Take away that reward and chances are you will take away the respect that we are in the process of building.

Back to, "Who am I?" Hopefully I have filled you in on how being wrong can be the best answer, provided we correct in the proper manner and allow our dogs the chance to prove and give us the right answer.

# Chapter 9:

# *Why Being Wrong Can Be Your Best Answer*

Having had as much opportunity as I have had to work with and help people become better and gain more experience in the dog world, has in itself been a fantastic experience to me. I usually tell my students at the clinics that I will probably learn the most, no matter how much I think I know. Something will come up and, through this, a new idea or piece to my training thoughts will have been answered. The more I think about such situations, the more it tells that when things go wrong it makes us think and in the process has me try new or different approaches. It is during such approaches that a new idea clicks which I am always ready to try; hence, another training experience is added. Being wrong to me is a positive way to becoming right.

My Dad would say being wrong is not all bad provided you think about it. If you think about it with a positive mind you will either

Jim at the ready as Jack gives a clinic in Lexington Virgina. Jim is owned by clinic host Nelly Bierly. *Photo by Tom Moates.*

learn from it or come up with the answer. If I were to come up with a fault in students at my clinics, this would be top of my list. Most of us are afraid to fail, and yet failure to me is not disaster. Failure means try again, think, and it will get better. When we are afraid to try, it means fear comes in, affects the mind, and makes answers hard to come by. I doubt I would have any students if they all knew how not to fail. Just as in many of my statements or sayings, relax, let the mind work, and don't worry about failing.

We are guilty of not thinking what it does to our dogs, when we are scared to try because we are afraid to fail. Right away you add that feeling to your dog. It can be in your tone of voice, it can be your hesitation to approach, it can be one of many different feelings we convey to our dog. Automatically the dog conveys that on to our sheep, which in turn either adds fear, or courage. To me failure should be something we learn to accept with the confidence that, if we think and try, we will figure this out and come up with an answer. There are many ways of being wrong or making a mistake, which, for me, can work towards my advantage just as much or possibly more than always being right.

I usually will think and dwell on the wrong, giving way for answers to come and to help right the wrong. When one is right, most of the time we give little thought to it. When I think about things like this, it often as not leads me to think about my dog or a dog. If this works for me why would it not be the same for the dog? I love to be able to see my dog's mind at work while giving corrections. A dog that is thinking about his correction usually comes up with his own reward. It's something for me that has become a very important part in my training, it builds a bond, respect for each other without even trying. It's funny why, talking about training, thinking about training may mean as much as the training itself. That's what helps me and my dogs "prepare." If we prepare, right answers come easy for dog and handler alike. If we push, demand, or try to make, that's when I find answers become difficult.

Being wrong for me means I must change. The first step is to admit that to oneself; once admitted is when I would start to try to solve the wrong. It's the same for my dog, if I can have my dog find his own wrong, through my correction it's like he has found his own answer. Yet, when I decide to make him right, I may get it but with a question mark. We all have our own ways of thinking and doing. That's why, for me, correct the wrongs and the real answers will follow. That's in some of my sayings "correct the wrong leave the right alone." Lots of people believe in praise for the right, but for me that takes away from a dog's mind what he achieved.

Another saying or belief of mine is "give the wrong the same chance as the right." Here again, if we give the wrong the same chance as the right, and are ready to correct if need be, the dog will correct himself rather than us making him right. It's all a philosophy of trying to use the dog's mind, as much as possible. A simple example would be on a recall. I see many people who own dogs and as long as everything is in control, everything looks good. But the second anything goes wrong, the bubble bursts. A good example of a dog being made right rather than one who was corrected and left with a choice is that the one who was made right, when released, takes off and gets out of the danger zone and his mind tells him "I'm free I can do what I want." Whereas the one who was corrected and is prepared right, when released, takes off and gets a correction, which right away triggers the mind to think, "what?" And the dog's mind will supply the answer.

# Chapter 10:

# Why The Use of the Mind Is So Important

The mind, its power, and why it's a leader for me is important to consider when we think of sheep dog trials. Not many people think about minds and yet there are so many used. We have the sheep's mind, we have the handler's mind, and we have the dog's mind. Then there is also the set-out crew's mind along with their dogs' minds. We have the judge's mind and of course we could go on and on. Let's look at some of those minds starting first with the sheep.

If the sheep are allowed to think, the chances are, if handled correctly, they will settle much the same as ourselves when we run our dogs. If the run goes well, we settle and most times do a pretty useful job. When things go wrong we panic, which brings fear, causes hesitation, and leaves the mind wondering what to do next. So where does the answer come from? The answer is the mind, a mind that asks what is causing the problem and how to try to solve it.

Most handlers today want their sheep at or as near the set out stake as possible. They do not take into account what is happening to the sheep's mind as the sheep are being set. Not only the sheep's mind but the mind of the set out crew and their dogs.

Another thing that comes into this picture is the course itself. This brings in more minds again, the people who pick the course and set it up. It's hard to set sheep correctly without the correct room to set them. Relaxing the sheep as we set them is very important and yet we don't always give the set out people the right to handle the sheep the way they should because we want them at that stake or near it. If we really think about some of this and use our minds correctly, I feel sheep would change. I feel it's very hard for a mind to change without a chance.

I remember going to southern California to judge a trial. When I got picked up at the airport, the early part of the conversation was how we needed to get back to the trial site. The sheep for the trial had arrived and they had not been worked with dogs. The idea was to go back and break the flock into small groups so as they would get used to dogs. We arrived back, and the working of the sheep started. As I watched, I could see that instead of calming or helping these sheep, the complete opposite was happening. Working the sheep was building fear instead of taking fear out. Upon my suggestion, we decided to leave the sheep as they were and that they would be fine. The moral of the story is they were great when handled correctly and a great trial followed.

For sheep to think, they need pressure taken off rather than pressure added. This allows the fear to leave and the mind to think. So setting sheep takes good stock sense rather than trying to make sheep be at a certain spot. Good stock sense comes from the setter who knows, who uses his mind to try to understand the sheep's mind—only adding pressure and taking pressure off when need be. Hence it should be up to the set-out crews how close they can set the sheep to the stake without upsetting them.

Jack oberves as an owner/handler attempts to send her dog around the sheep. *Photo by Tom Moates.*

We are guilty of using our minds sometimes to get what we want rather than what we need. The dog's mind is controlled a lot in the same way. The pressure of the sheep has a way of upsetting or settling the dog. Say the sheep are flighty or scared; we must keep our dog way off or stop him to take the pressure off, which in the process frees the mind to think. As the sheep thinks, provided the dog stays put or gives enough freedom, then both minds start to work giving a feel between dog and sheep. A fast dog or a hyper dog is likely to cause more problems between sheep and dog.

This is where handling correctly comes in the picture. It's critical for a handler to stay calm so as to allow his mind to make right and clear decisions so as to help sheep and dog alike. Looking at the handler's mind, I don't know about others but it's easy for me to see after the run some of the mistakes made by not thinking. The judge's mind comes into this picture as well. As we talk about setting sheep, a good judge will take into his judgment where handler and dog picked the sheep up, how far they were off line, and whether the dog had a fair chance at his lift and a chance to hit his fetch gates. It's the judge's mind that has to make all these decisions. He may have 70 or 80 dogs to judge; one has to be very careful in allowing a rerun. The judge may allow a rerun only if he feels that the dog and handler did not have a fair chance. The mind is as important in sheep dog trialing as it is in training a sheep dog. Allowing animals to think is what clears the mind much the same as it does for ourselves.

When we think in general about our own minds, it's the same answer. Say we are angry about something. If we went to write down at the time what we thought or what the mind was telling us, then went back later when the anger had left with the pressure off the mind, I feel most of our answers would be very different. If we were scared, the fear would affect our thoughts, often lead us to panic, and naturally lead us to make wrong decisions.

The mind is a leader; it controls the body and even controls how we use it; panic, fear, hate, trust, feel, the list is endless. Let's say I hate something or someone, how is the easy way to start correcting that? By thinking about it and letting our minds work. Let's start on ourselves. What is causing the hate? Is it something we don't like or something that happened to cause us to not like someone? The easy way to go is to let the mind blame someone else for the wrong. The real answer is to look at our own minds and ask why do we have to feel that way. If we think, we can forgive, we can correct, we can take pressure off our mind and get the answer. When one feels that relief, it is a positive answer and in many cases goes on to solve the whole problem. It's no different for the dog or the sheep.

# Chapter 11:

# Fun

What's fun for our dogs? For me, the best fun is something unexpected. In other words, not planned, not made, just something that happens. I watch and observe dogs and people and their differences in what fun is for themselves and their dogs, and it teaches me what I don't want for my dog.

After a thirteen-hour trip, I watched friends as they took their dogs out to walk them. This gave me fire to write this chapter. There was nothing unusual about this, other than the reaction of the dogs. For me, they were not out for a walk or a run, but a chase. I watched as the dogs ran, chased, and I suppose in their own mind had fun. This put my mind to work. I started thinking about the possible benefits of the exercise, then the possible disadvantages, and to be honest, for me the wrongs outnumbered the rights.

It reminded me of the days when I would go out and think I had fun and instead the next day wonder why I had done what I

Jack allows his own dogs freedom during a break at a clinic.
*Photo by Tom Moates.*

had done. Dogs that come out of their kennel and stop, look, and ask "what are we doing?" are the ones I look for. They are asking, thinking, waiting, wondering: are we going for a walk, to work, or maybe just out to go potty? At least they are thinking and if left alone will come up with their own answers. If an answer is wrong, I will correct, and if right, I'll leave them alone. To the dog that comes out excited and is asked, "Are you ready to get out? Bill, was it a long ride?" in a tone that makes him happy, only adds to the excitement and takes away the mind. I always believe a dog left to think, if corrected in the right manner, will find the right answer. If not, he is prepared to think when given the correction.

Dogs are no different from people. When we are excited or angry, most of the time we don't use our minds to our best advantage. I know for myself most of the time when I have been mad at my dog, or too excited about the answer—in other words, over praised or made too much fuss over the dog—I feel later that I have taken away from that dog rather than given to him. Let's say I let my dogs out for a walk; as I approach the kennel if I start making too much fuss by asking them how they are today, asking if they are ready to get out, and creating excitement in my dogs before letting them out, I am only making my dogs hyper. I would be setting them up to be excited, to run, to chase, and have their minds in the wrong mode. Instead, I feel my dogs are happier if, when I approach and they are getting excited, I say "What's going on?" or "Hey." That correction calms the mind.

For me, each time I prepare my dog's mind to think, it gets its answers much easier. By exciting a dog too much with unnecessary praise we are building the dog's excitement and putting the mind in the wrong mode rather than using a correction or calming tone, which will have our dog more prepared. People may read this chapter and ask "what has all this got to do with training a dog?" For my method or way of training, I feel we must look for an open mind in our dogs which will give them the chance to accept corrections. Time has taught me that the easy way to a dog's heart is through the mind allowing him to give rather than me trying to make. To achieve this goal we have to correct enough to have our dog think and, most important, be ready to accept the answer.

Thinking of giving rather than making brings another story to mind. After a three day clinic, on my journey home, I travelled and spent the night at a friend's home. On the following morning as I was shown around the property we had this young dog, Jim, along. He was on a long line and behaving, I would say, exceptionally well. As we approached the first gate I watched with interest as my friend approached with the dog. Before he opened the gate he said, "Jim, lie down, stay," then opened the gate and asked Jim to come, lie down, stay, then closed it. We proceeded to the second gate with much the same ritual.

As we went on to the next gate I said to my friend, "Were you not at a Jack Knox Clinic this past weekend?"

She replied with a puzzled look on her face, "Yes, why?"

I said, "did you not hear the words 'freedom for the dog?'"

Again she replied, "Yes, why?"

I said, "At the next gate, I'll take Jim, just watch."

So as we approached the gate I took Jim, went to the gate, and as it opened, Jim went to dive through. I gave a quick correction and a firm tone "Jim!" and the dog gave. I stepped back through, took off the line, and said, "Watch."

As I approached and opened the gate the dog started to make his move, I gently said "Jim" in a low but firm manner and the dog just stopped. The dog moved with me as I stepped forward and back. Jim was giving to me, not being made to sit, stay, come, all on commands, but giving, finding his own answer how to give, not being made to.

As we proceeded on our way to the house I said to my friend, "I know where you got your method."

She asked, "How do you know that?

I said, "Never mind how I know, figure out which is the best way and use it."

As we walked I asked, "Why is Jim on this line?"

She said, "Because he will take off, run to the sheep, come back, and have fun in his own way."

I released Jim and as the line came off I gave another firm and positive correction. Jim relaxed and we continued on our walk, with the occasional correction; Jim a contented dog with a happy owner.

# Chapter 12:

# Jack's Teacher Makes an Impact

Trying to make dogs better than they are is one mistake I feel I have made over and over. I still feel I fall into the same bracket sometimes while I train my dogs. I know what I want, but at the same time, I don't take into consideration what my dog is thinking.

Sometimes I want a dog to down, and when he won't, I will apply pressure until I get that answer, never considering what my dog is going through in the process. For me, this gives me an answer but leaves the dog without one. If one takes the time to study these dogs and really trusts them, I feel this is the wrong practice. It's better to work this dog, find ways where you can read his mind, and ease him or her into the position where he or she is more likely to want to down. It's all about getting the dog to want to give to you rather than to make him.

A dog is like a person; when we can give a friend the help he or she needs without being asked, it makes us feel good and also our friend appreciates it more. It's like a bad flank; it's not the end of the world and chances are with a little help it is going to get better. So say on the bad flank, next time we flank this dog, maybe we say his name or draw his attention just a little before asking. If there's a change, no matter how small, it's working, just give it time. Trying to rush that answer adds pressure and confuses the mind.

The real fun in training dogs is when they are showing us what they have to offer. So often we are in too big of a hurry to even look for the small insights to allow them to mature. I see this at clinics over and over; someone's dog shows great change so they want to work it more. Luckily, time does not allow this. Maybe next time out, the same dog shows nervousness or fear and people lose faith in what they just saw. We have got to have in mind what our dog is thinking. The dog just got a glimmer of that change, but there are lots of things taking up the dog's mind at this time, whether it be fear, uncertainty, whatever, but if we will wait, the dog will come back to that change and be even better. We are very guilty of not waiting on our dog to give us its best answer. The more I watch people and their dogs, the more this approach becomes important.

It's like when we give a correction and the dog turns off or sulks, then we tend to panic. If a correction is given correctly, then it's up to the dog to figure that answer out; maybe not today, but maybe two days from now. The dog that figures out the correction and its meanings is the dog I would want to end up with. A correction has to be meant for the answer to come out; this does not mean it has to be hard or severe.

I often tell a story at clinics of a school teacher I had when I was ten or twelve years old. Although he will never know, he has played a very important role in my life. First, he was a man of dignity, pride, and respect; one whose classroom behavior was beyond the best. I can see him yet, walking in that door and silence would be instant.

He was a teacher very well liked by us kids but one who stood no nonsense. I can remember him to this day as he walked up and down the classroom; if you had done anything wrong, whisper to a friend, try to copy someone else's answers, he would just walk by and as he did, just rap you over the knuckles with his ruler which was a 12 inch measuring stick. I can still feel some of these corrections to this day. But if I could meet teacher Ted tomorrow, I would thank him, not only for the correction but also for what it has meant to me in life.

Some may wonder what this has to do with training dogs. All I can tell them is, "far more than they will ever know." For me, a lot of lessons learned in everyday life have opened up answers while I train my dogs. The correction given by teacher Ted was firm, positive, and left our minds thinking on our wrongs. He would never stop to explain why, just expect a change. With a positive correction, the mind gives its own answer. It's not the correction that works, it's the freedom behind it; at least it seemed to work for me. I feel my dogs deserve that same choice. Dogs, again, are like people; they love to please, they love to give, therefore giving the choice opens up that door.

# Chapter 13:

# Feelings

The longer I work with dogs, the more I feel relationship plays an important part. So why relationship, what is it, and why is it so important?

First of all, a good relationship is based on feelings which for me is so important. Let's think of ourselves, our family, as an example. My wife, what she thinks, how she acts, happy, angry, sad, all affect how I feel. My daughter, Kate, if she is bothered, wants something she does not need, or is over excited about something, these are all things that affect how I feel. Friends, and even acquaintances, make us think and they all bring out different feelings. These feelings generally bring out how we relate to how others act.

So back to dogs, many people never consider how their dog acts. If the act is pleasing to them, they are too busy praising. If the dog is doing the wrong thing, I find they are more determined to make them right rather than to ask themselves the question why. If

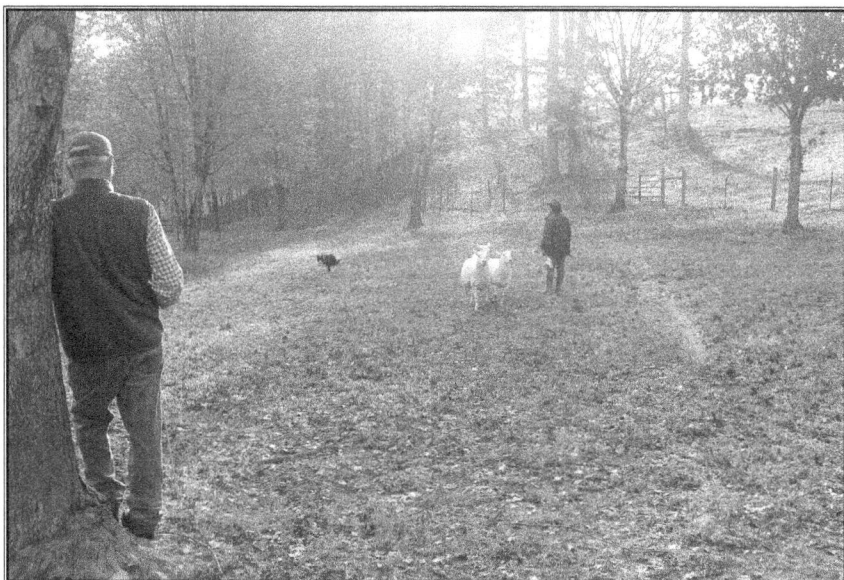

This dog guides the sheep towards the handler giving freedom on the flank which allows the sheep to think and stay calm as they are turned around the handler's feet. *Photo by Tom Moates.*

we look at why, then we may be able to help rather than make the answer.

To help, I want a good relationship with my dog. That means he knows when I am mad or knows when I am happy. The dog should read my feelings: disappointed, sad, or excited. To me, many people don't take time to understand how important this is to the dog. A dog that understands, that trusts, that knows when we are happy, accepts how we feel; that's the dog with the right relationship and is ready to train. When I think of feelings, it brings out how much, if we use them correctly, we can learn. When used the wrong way, meaning that I think everyone else is wrong and I am right, one has nothing to gain. Looking for the wrong is easy if we correct ourselves. Not so much so if we allow the mind to rule our answer. It's taken many years for me to understand that being wrong is not all bad and that straightening out one's wrongs gives good honest answers. It's just another lesson these dogs have taught me.

To allow a dog to use its honest feelings, we have to open up the wrong for them to experience rather than prevent it from happening. Gone are the days for me when I have to put a leash on the dog to take it to sheep, when I have to step out in front of it to get it to go around, or when I have to run at it or force the stop. Get the basics right first so your dog understands, then step out of its way and give freedom. This allows me to see what to correct. I watch people with dogs on a leash who have to lay the dog down so as they can take the leash off. To me, this is control not freedom. I want to switch this around where my dog wants to give rather than me having to make him. A dog with feelings, that has been taught the correct way, takes little to correct. Dogs made or forced either get scared or excited which makes them tough to correct because the basics are not there. Feelings are no different in dogs than they are in ourselves. When we are nervous or scared it's hard to think; putting pressure on ourselves only makes us worse.

Let's take this dog that has been controlled; how can we change him? My first step would be allowing him the freedom to be wrong. If the wrong takes over then we need our correction enforced. When this fails it tells me the correction is not being understood or that the dog is ignoring it. Then I would take a step back and work on my basics.

I get many dogs at my clinics that, when released, completely ignore corrections. You might ask why? Because they have never been taught not to. All their life they have been controlled. It's what the dog feels that matters, not if the dog is happy or not. Let's look at the dog that, in the owner's mind, is wonderful, yet when the owner goes to take the leash off he has to control. Compare this to the dog who has been taught the basics correctly and has the choice of freedom so if he does wrong a small correction will give the mind a change and give the dog a chance to answer. Which way is more fair?

There is no doubt in my mind, the dog allowed freedom to think and taught to understand will work to please giving the owner and the dog a positive answer. That is the relationship between dog and owner. It's what the dogs feel about a correction that counts. If they understand the correction then they should feel the reward on the tone of the handler's voice. It's huge for dog and owner alike and another reason for me to thank these dogs for their excellent reactions which continue to teach and amaze me more not only about their capabilities, but about life in general. Having my dog's feelings right makes training easy. It's better to have one feel the wrong and try to correct than have to make the answer.

# Chapter 14:

# Relationship

This may seem funny to many, but for me relationship is most important whether it be with my wife, my friend, or my daughter. Why am I writing about relationship when this book is supposed to be about dogs? I believe more and more that the bond between me and my dogs is as important as the training.

Let's look at relationship, and I will try to relate what it means for me. First, I do not believe we can make relationships but, rather, we build them. What does it involve? I believe trust, respect, caring, and believing in each other is what relationships are built from. Back to my dogs, I often think of the way I raise pups. My pups are loved, respected, and corrected when wrong, but not over praised when right. It's just me in my everyday life spending time with my best friends. It's not about what they give, it's more about who they really are: honest, trustworthy, faithful, ready to defend themselves when in need but, at the same time, willing to give in if wrong! All of these qualities are important for me in a dog.

I teach my dogs to accept a correction while I am ready to correct myself if wrong. I don't believe in over praising. I try to build that bond between my dog and myself that we respect each other and, if anything, over try for each other. I watch people over praise and yet, the minute they are not happy, talk to their dog as if it were dirt. For me, if I were a dog, I would just hate that. I feel it's when things go wrong that we need the praise. It's the "okay buddy, I know you were trying" attitude that builds a relationship. I often wonder what the dogs thinks when we talk to them in these negative terms. I know, for me, it would be hard to forget. Certainly not the way I want my dog to feel in our relationship. I do feel it's just as important for our dogs to believe in us, to trust us, and to respect us. At the end of the day, we are there to honor each other for our try and there to support each other if we fail.

I see too many people fuss too much over their dogs. It's as if they believe "the more I do for you, the better you will be to me." Let's look at that in our everyday life. Say we give a kid $5.00 to mow the yard. He is pretty excited about the money. Then after a while, he wants $10.00 and so it goes on. Compare this to the kid who volunteers to mow. He mows and thinks to himself, he missed a little piece on the edge. When he sees this, he goes back and corrects, finishes mowing, looks again, and is proud of the job he has done. He might even look forward to mowing the next time. The difference, number one, is mowing the yard for the reward or, in other words, what he wants. Number two, he is doing the job for what he can give and achieves his contentment by what he gives, plus the pride in how he gives. When I sum up these differences and compare them to dog training, I would shoot for number two. Number one, he got what he wanted to have, and number two, he achieved his need by giving.

When I compare this to training my own dogs it is the same. Say I go out with my first dog, I lie him down, move away to make distance between me and my dog, and then, as I send him I add

At a clinic in Lexington Jack discusses why he is not in favor of using a flag or tools for his method of training. *Photo by Tom Moates.*

force to make my answer. In my mind that is making the dog do what I ask. The difference is, as I go out with my second dog, I will achieve the better answer without making, but instead by correcting. It is sometimes hard for people to understand that by allowing a wrong, it makes it easier for the dog to find the right. As I go out with my number two dog, I send him and, as I do, move away from him leaving freedom for the wrong or right. If he is right, I leave the dog alone, but the second he goes wrong, I correct. It may take one or two attempts for the dog to understand, but as the correction becomes clearer, the answers become more positive.

The number one dog succeeds because we made him. The number two dog succeeds because of the wrong we helped him correct, which leaves a completely different mindset in each dog.

The number two dog got his answer by us helping him find his wrong and in the process gave me, as the trainer, satisfaction that he found his answer through using his mind. Two minds working for each other is what builds trust and forms the relationship I look for in my dog. The number one dog, on the other hand, was made to do what my mind wanted which, in the process, took away the chance from my dog to use and correct his own mind. It's allowing minds to work, to think, to correct, and to respect that builds relationship.

I still get amazed at my own pups and dogs as relationships build. I have two puppies right now that are four months or so. They are treated like my older dogs, but puppies being puppies they want to run, play, and chase, which annoys me. I am usually shouting or correcting and it's funny because they are just right now at that point of change. They will run and chase each other, and I may yell their names as a correction. I'll watch them give, think, and then maybe want to go back to chase. The next time I just say the name and watch as they figure this out.

They are the same on the sheep. I may take one at night with two or three of my trained dogs to fetch in ewes and lambs. A week or ten days ago they might have done quite a silly chase but now, as they do, I speak and they draw up, think, and are beginning to find their answers. They are starting to show a little eye and balance, all of which is basically self-taught. As the respect and the trust grows between us, so will our relationship.

It's the same with sheep, and I'm sure many of you will be asking, "how can we find a relationship with sheep?" I think it's real easy if people go out and study their sheep; they will find the sheep, in return, will study them. But instead, we go out to work and feed and nine times out of ten don't take the time to give the sheep a chance. If you are real observant, you will see certain dogs that have a great influence on sheep. The sheep can change for that dog all because of the contact and how the dog uses it. Sometimes I feel we do not pay enough attention to things like that. We are too busy trying to achieve what we want. Again, this is relationship between sheep, dog, and people. I want to finish this off by explaining about a photo I have of my dog "Jim" after winning the Soldier Hollow Trial. I had just made my pen, took off my hat to acknowledge the crowd, leaned down to acknowledge Jim, and the look on his face said it all: "We did it, master."

When I think back on my life today, the ups the downs, the rights the wrongs, most of the time I'll go back to my wrongs in life. For me, it's the wrongs corrected that makes life better. The rights, yes they are nice to think about, but only to make one feel good. The wrongs corrected are what give answers. The longer I live, the more I think about this and the more I realize the importance.

The wrong once done stays wrong, even if we change. Again, you may ask, "What has this to do with dogs?" For me, it was the dogs that taught me this. Watching them change from wrong to right, seeing the dog realize it is wrong, studying my dog's reactions, and how it changed made the answer easy for me to see that change. It's when our dogs give us something like this that we should be ready to give back. Not praise and tell him how good he was, but feed him more of what he is succeeding with. For me, this is what our dogs love. They want to give, and as they do when given the chance to use their minds, can feel in themselves the answers they are giving to us. I believe they can read for themselves the pride, respect, and trust we feel as our dogs give us their all. This is what I feel builds the bond to true relationship between my dog and me.

# Chapter 15:

# Natural Versus Trainer Made

This may be a matter of choice in training, but I thought I would add my thoughts on the idea of natural versus trainer made and what I believe we are taking away from our dogs. I am one who believes in correcting wrongs to find rights, rather than preventing wrongs. It is my honest opinion that by making our dogs right we are taking away some of the better values which handlers and shepherds of the past bred into and built to give these Border Collies the brains, feelings, eye, balance, and style which make them what they are today.

What is the difference and why do I feel so strongly in this field? First of all, it's these dogs that have made me into who I am today. They have given me the chance in life to advance, the opportunity in life to travel—the education in life they have given me is unbelievable. When I think of all that these wonderful dogs have given and done for me, they are still, after a lifetime of education and enjoyment, teaching me, if anything, more today than ever before. Why? It's because I understand them so much better. The reason I have greater understanding is because I think more. Not thoughts about how to up the training, but thoughts on how they are keeping me thinking and opening my mind to new ideas.

It's just amazing for me while I work with dogs—be it my own or other people's dogs—the real answers I come up with. The dogs teach me when I am wrong, which in turn gets my mind working trying to find a way to allow the dog's mind to come up with a better answer. We seem to forget it's the dogs that we have bred with exceptional minds, and yet we feel like our mind knows more. Stop and think about it, and for me this all makes sense. When it comes to training, if we as handlers think we know and make these dogs follow our thoughts, we leave the best part out, which is their breeding.

Let's start with the puppy; it's either spoiled and gets its own way because it's just a puppy, or it is shut in the kennel and in some ways put aside until training commences. Puppies are like little kids, they can tell us a lot if we give them a chance, correct their wrongs, and watch their answers. One can be taught what one can see from a pup in its early childhood.

When we start our dogs, how we want control with a down or a recall, all these are things a pup can learn on its own if corrected in the right manner. Same with the outrun; how we position ourselves in front of our dog so he has to give left or right provides pressure to the mind to make him correct. It goes from here to forcing him out, more to satisfy our minds and get him to the position we want, rather than giving the dog the chance and only using pressure when he or she is wrong and allowing our dog to correct itself. It's the same with flanks, force versus being asked. All of these things come down to training and how each individual trains. But if we think about this, the one way is about "do as I say or else." The other is "ask" and correct, and as the answer comes, it's the dog's mind that gives the answer.

It's my idea that by making our dogs do as we think, we are taking away the dog's mind and natural ability. A natural dog with good feel is the one who passes on the genes to breed better dogs, not the dog which through training goes on to be a winner mostly because a person has trained or molded the dog to make him into the dog he is. Just remember, most people buy or breed because of winners, which in some way I understand, but the question I ask myself is, was the winner justified? Did he or she have the things I like to see in my dog, or was the dog just well trained and shown to perfection? When I stop and think about all of this I keep coming up with the same answer. Who taught me to think this way? The dogs.

Looking back, I was very much one who thought I knew the way to train and make dogs better. Little did I know that my future was to change and that the dogs would become my guides. It's all due to the mind change these dogs passed on to me that has changed, improved, and made me into who I am today. It's been a wonderful journey with no end in sight.

Pride in one's work, the words come easy, but as I watch, think, and ponder on what pride is all about, so many real answers come through. When I look back on what we were taught in life about pride and all its meanings, compared to today, it in some ways makes me sad. We are in too big of a hurry. "It does not matter; what difference will it make," and more of an attitude of "I don't care" prevails. But when one stops and analyzes what pride really conveys, the answers are endless, both for our dogs and us. I always convey to my students that doing things the right way, rather than the easy way or taking shortcuts, will tell its tale in success. Pride is such a big part in these statements.

Looking back on pictures of trials and handlers years ago tells its own story of pride—handlers, by the way they were dressed to go to trials: collar, tie, polished boots, proud to be out there showing off their pride and joy. I can remember talking to people like the late John Gilchrist on why he did not take a shed or try to hurry to beat the clock. His answer was simple yet positive, "If you can't do the job right, you should not be out there." A far cry from today, running in the shedding ring, slamming the pen gate, rushing to get what points we can while getting finished whatever way possible. Yes, we have taken away the pride, class, dignity, respect, that sheep dog trials once had.

It's funny; for me sheepdog trials long ago were something I looked forward to and enjoyed. This enjoyment could be running my dog, or watching others. I must have gone to more trials just to watch than ever I have run in, and yet I can honestly say I enjoyed them every bit as much. That's changed today, not only in myself but I hear the same from others. So what's the difference? You take class, dignity, honor, and respect away from anything and you will destroy much of the desire for whatever it be to succeed. Our trials today are bigger. We build them up more. We are never satisfied, always wanting better sheep, judges, dogs, water on the course, one could go on and on. The cost of putting on trials keeps soaring, yet we don't want to change or think that if we stepped back in time and looked at what trials represented, we could find quite a few answers.

Sheep, for example, they are becoming harder to find. Yes, there are not the numbers there once were, but do we take care of the sheep we get? We make sure they are fed and watered and normally have a vet available, but on course they are not handled, or steered, like long ago. Sheep are not thought of, respected, and treated anywhere near what they were in the past. We don't have pride in them, otherwise sheep would be our first concern.

Our dogs may get the job done better than the others; however it does not matter any more if it's right, as long as it's better. Handlers' attitudes today are a far cry from what they were back then. We don't appreciate things half as much like "the honor" and "chances" that we are given as the people did of long ago. Long ago, folks and handlers alike appreciated having the chance to visit or compete in trials. They were willing to support and do what was needed to see them survive. Today, we want sponsors, pay setouts while we complain at the smallest faults and, in truth, believe everything should be done for us. Maybe it's just me or that I am getting old, but I honestly feel, if we showed a little of our pride, rebuilt a bit of our dignity, showed a little more class, the respect of what we do in trials and the "honor" of how we gain respect, could go a long way in how our trials survive in the future.

# Chapter 16:

# Making The Commands Easier

This is something that I have found to be useful in my training. As an example, let's look at the down command. Most people approach a dog or put pressure on a dog to achieve the down. As most of us know, this procedure works and trains a dog to down. So, why do I question this? It's not that I feel it's so wrong as much as I appose the side effects it can cause.

For me, as I watch and study my dog, I notice that when I ask for that stop or down, the dog through eagerness does not want to give it. As I raise my voice and change my tone, the dog might show a sign of fear or move off my correction. This in some ways is fine, as they are giving me their answer. However, through observing I have found that for the dog's benefit a little extra help on this can be to my dog's advantage.

Sometimes with a dog like this I use a line. As I enforce the pressure and my dog shows fear or awareness, I add pressure with the line, just enough to have the dog think. This would be enough to keep him from moving away from the pressure but at the same time not causing him more fear. This procedure I would do without sheep. It's something one has to be real patient with and allow the dog to understand the difference between tone change and anger. It's what I call "building the trust between dog and handler." I find that certain dogs need this help.

There are many other small things that can make huge changes in a dog. Teaching a dog to give to sheep rather than making him give is another example. I do a lot of this when I am first starting my dogs. I start most of them in a small area, preferably a ring of about 50 or 60 feet in diameter. As the sheep move, the dog's first move is either to chase or herd. How the dog approaches the sheep will define how I react. Most of my dogs at this stage pretty much understand my tones, something I am a big believer in. As this dog approaches and is coming hard, my tone would be high and harsh to the point where the instant that dog changed, and by changed I mean any change, I would give and allow him his sheep again. This I would keep up until my dog was feeling the change the same as I did; in other words, both minds would be at work, rather than one trying to make the other.

The same on the dog with less aggression, the one who is more inclined to herd or balance. I would still use my tones, but in a sweeter or milder fashion. By doing this I find that trust and respect begin growing between the dog and me. After each correction I begin to see the dog think more. If he gives, I give and our minds satisfy each other. It's an exercise that most people, if they start, don't take time to finish. It's very important that your dog is allowed time to give you his or her answer. You need to wait on your dog. As this exercise or training continues I would develop it to where I can pull my dog in on sheep or ask him out. This is a huge benefit for dogs in their later training when I begin opening flanks, opening outruns, correcting tightness at the top, the pen, or the shed. It's some of the basics that give opportunities for dogs to show their talents in the later stages. Small practices such as this can take pressure off a dog's mind, and it's always rewarding for me to see the change in my dog when he is free to think.

Excitement follows in the same way. For me, excited dogs never act right because they don't think right. Yet this is the first thing we tend to do with our pup. It's all about praise; we tell them "you are beautiful, have fun, you are just a pup." Most things we say to our puppies are praise or make excuses for their wrongs and excite them. We try to make them happy and allow them to have fun; that's what pups are all about. Well that may be true to lots of folks but, for me, I would question it. I think of people and what praise means to them, I watch kids and what praise means to them, and finally I analyze what it means to me.

When I was growing up, my father would encourage rather than praise. Oh, I would know he was proud of me, but he always left me with the thought of how much. In other words, left my mind to figure that out, kept me thinking rather than making me excited. He or my family would be more ready to discourage me for being a bad sport or for not trying hard enough. In other words, they kept me on an even keel. I usually knew by their actions how they felt which, in turn, was encouragement for me without the praise to excite. Many of these lessons I think of and watch in our kids today. We are praising kids for trying, not just for succeeding. It's surprising to me to hear people say how they have to take time off work. Their nights are all taken up, as they have to go support the children. Long ago, that was impossible; time would not allow it and parents could not afford it. Yet when I think of it all, there are no parents more proud of their kids than mine were, and yet all the years I played rugby and other sports in school I never remember my Dad being present. The point I am trying to make is he did not have to be there, but I knew he was there in his mind. A great gift he passed on to me that I value very highly to this day.

I associate much of my upbringing as a big part of where I am in the success the dogs have given to me. Many of the tools of my trade come from the way my father molded me into who I am today. I often wonder if he knew how special he was and how great were the great gifts he left. Going back to excitement, for me it's about finding a way to convey to our animals how good, how right, how great they are doing, without the use of too much praise. Praise is something we all like but in most cases is unnecessary. For me, it lights a candle in the mind, which leads to excitement. A calm mind that thinks is better than a hyper or excited one.

People who read this they may get the feeling I am a mean or selfish person. It's amazing as I watch dogs how they respect and look up to me for who I am. Teaching as many clinics as I do and seeing other handlers' dogs who want to give, who are happy to be around me, tells my how when I give the dog what he needs he, in turn, will give to me all he's got. It's kind of like a special friend; I don't have to give them anything special, they are my friend for what I am and what I mean to them.

# Chapter 17:

# Raising Puppies

Everybody has his or her own way of handling dogs or raising puppies. Raising a puppy is like raising a child, correct the wrong and leave the right. I think far too many people want to praise or spoil puppies too much. There's nothing wrong with loving the pup and letting it know rights from wrongs. For me, what I want to do is raise a pup up to respect me. How do you go about getting a puppy to respect you? You correct its wrongs and let it think about what the right is. The more it thinks about it, the more answers it gets, and the more it respects the person who's doing the correcting to give it these answers.

It's pretty interesting to watch people who raise a pup; often they spoil the pup as they grow up yet are mad at the same pup later on. They don't understand that spoiling puppies so much causes them to be wrong. They didn't teach the puppy to think for himself in the first place.

I always tell people at my clinics, when you see someone get a new puppy, the first thing the owner does is pick it up. You have to love it, hug it, spoil it, buy a leash for it, get a fancy collar for it, and basically put the puppy in prison. When I get a puppy, I want to give him freedom. Why do I want to give the puppy freedom? I want to see what it wants to do, then I know what to correct and what to leave alone.

When the puppy is left alone and I think he is doing right, I might encourage him; I might praise him. I don't go overboard with my praise; I want the puppy to be thinking about what he does. When the puppy is doing wrong, I correct. How do I correct? I correct with the tone of my voice. If a puppy is doing wrong, I might say, "Aggh." And if he didn't listen, I'd say, "Hey!" and be more abrupt or use a more firm tone to correct. I let the puppy read the tone much the same as you read music. Music is all about tone, so changing my tone can sound like music to that pup. That's letting the mind work, that's letting the brain think, that's giving the puppy a chance to correct itself. Puppies are just like a person; they love when they feel that correction work; they love to get better. I think a lot of people seem to misunderstand that part, but for me it's something that's important.

I explain it at clinics: I always tell people, you know if you're walking a puppy and you have him on a leash, the first thing he wants to do is chew on your shoelace because of the movement. When he starts chewing on my shoelace, I would bend down and say, "no." If he didn't listen, I would correct him. How would I correct him? I might pinch his ear and he might give me an answer like "oh, I didn't like that." The next time he decided to chew my shoelace and I corrected him, he might look up at me as much to say, "what?" With just that simple exercise, the puppy is asking what you want rather than you making it do what you want. I think there's so much difference in that.

That's the big difference I've found in training dogs and how dogs get answers and start to respect their owners and trainers. They start answering because you gave them a chance. The other way is when the puppy does wrong a lot of people bend down and pick the puppy up and say, "well, you weren't supposed to do that," shake the puppy and put him down again, but there would really be no answer in that. You're not correcting the mistake. You might be correcting the puppy, but the puppy doesn't understand it. You have to try to correct so that the puppy understands; it's much easier for that dog. If you start correcting the puppy the proper way, you'll find that, as he grows up and you start to train him, he'll give you far more answers. The reason being is you've taught him to think.

When I raise puppies, I try to let puppies grow up as soon as they can. I give them the option of moving from the puppy shelter into the kennel. Why do I do that? Because when I was a little boy, I wanted to be like the grownups. I think that puppy deserves the same chance. So when he does get the chance to go into the kennel, the first thing I try to look for is behavior. That doesn't mean I go and make him behave all the time, but I would correct if he is barking or whining. I would go back and I would talk to him. If he didn't listen, the correction would be firmer. If he didn't take the correction, he would get another one. As soon as I see any reaction from that puppy, then he gets freedom. It's not that I make him stop—I correct and then give him a chance to think and grasp onto that. If he doesn't understand, then my corrections become more determined and more firm. You'll find that soon that puppy will start to be proud of his correction. He'll start to sit in the kennel and look for you to come. When you come, he'll look at you as much as to say, "What are we going to do?" That's a thinking dog. That's a puppy being taught the right way.

The difference, the other way, is when you go in the kennel and you say, "Oh, how are you today?" and talk to the puppy, getting your puppy all excited. That puppy is not thinking. You're making him hyper, you're making him—I wouldn't say crazy—but you're making the mind run at an exciting pace rather than a thinking pace. Instead, you want to try to keep your dogs thinking. That's what the pup likes to do, that's what we like to do as people. When we are thinking about something, time passes by fast compared to when we are sitting doing nothing; we get bored. When we're excited and not thinking, we're being silly. It's the same thing with the dog.

These are just a few things I look for in a pup as that pup grows up and starts to show more of the dog in himself. When I do take that puppy out and he's running and chasing and doing something wrong, I speak to him and he'll think and say, "What?" At this stage, I would ask again, and if no response he gets a firmer correction. When the correction is accepted, the puppy will then answer through the choice of freedom, not force.

To me, too many people begin making corrections on their pup far too late. If you leave that puppy till he is six months old, remember he's got longer legs, he'll be much harder to catch, therefore making him harder to correct. Then you have to start making rather than asking and you take the freedom of choice away from that pup.

When I take him out, if he's doing something wrong, I yell his name. I say, "Bob, Bob!" and if he listens and gives me any inclination he's trying to listen at all, I let him go. I would never think of correcting him to make him listen unless the dog did not answer. I just work on that and get that answer more positive instead of praising him when he's right, which stops the mind working. You've got to remember, when you praise you stop the mind; you make them exited. You make them feel good. I want them to feel good because they are using their minds. I want the dog to find that answer. I want the dog to read what I'm thinking. If you think about that statement, "I want the dog to read what I'm thinking," that's the dog using its mind, not our mind. It's not using its mind when you're getting the pup excited or praising it. It's not using its mind when it's scared to death because you're going to make it do something. That's using the mind the wrong way. A dog that thinks and gives you answers is way ahead of the dog that is made to give answers.

When I raise a puppy I expect it to know three main things. First is the name; that's the first thing I start to teach it. I say, "Puppy, puppy," and then "Bill, Bill, Bill." Once it starts to learn its name, a correction would be the next thing I would teach it. I also want to have the pup come when I call it. All these would be taught together. When the puppy is right, I might call it. If it listens, that's good, but if it doesn't listen, then a correction is needed. I want the pup to know its name, understand corrections, and also be able to recall. That's all I care about on a puppy. I don't care about downs and other commands of "do this, do that." I don't believe in making the puppy do it.

What I do like to teach a puppy is tones. When he is wrong, for example, I might say, "Hey, hey, hey, hey!" and just make the tone to where the puppy would give to me. The same if the puppy is doing good, "Atta boy, come on, Bill, Bill, Bill." That puppy will learn from my tone without me telling him if he's a good boy. He'll know he's right. I think tone is very, very important. Same in my recall. If I'm recalling a puppy and he's not listening, I don't keep praising him.

A lot of people try to call a puppy using the wrong tone. If the puppy doesn't listen say, "Hey, come on you." That's asking her or him to come. That pup will pick up a whole lot through tone. It's very, very important. The commands are the three I told you: the name, the correction, and the recall. That's all I want in my young pups. That's all I try to teach them before I start a new training program.

Raising a puppy the right way is often overlooked. This is just an example of what I like. I remember being at a clinic one Sunday afternoon when this lady brought out a puppy at the lunch break.

He was a very well marked, a pretty little pup, and well behaved. Of course everybody was oohing over this pup, and it was being handed around from person to person, being petted and praised and hugged—you name it, they did it. After they were all finished, the puppy was laid down on the ground and we were all standing talking. Of course I was talking away, but I was also paying attention to that puppy.

The puppy would run up and it might sniff at the grass, it might go to the bathroom. It would run along and it would look at something, then it would turn its head and it would do something else. It might run over to the gate and look under the gate when it saw the sheep move. It might prick its ears and be interested. Everything that puppy did, it told me it was thinking. So when I started the clinic that day, I said to the clinic participants, "You've all been watching this pup, and you've all been admiring this pup. Some of you have been hugging this pup and petting this pup, but when did you see the puppy learning the most?"

Nobody even saw it; they never saw the puppy doing all the thinking for himself, putting himself in a position to be corrected. If you go back to what I've been saying, when you're holding the puppy and petting him and exciting him, you can't correct him for anything. If you let a puppy run loose, and he's running about doing things right, I leave him alone. But say he wanted to chase a cat if it runs across the yard, I would say, "Hey!" If he didn't listen, I would run and chase him and I'd make him listen. I would correct him for not listening. That's what I think is the best way to raise pups. This is something that is obvious to me. It stood out at that clinic; people were amazed when I said it. They often don't think to look for that.

It's the same thing with the bold pup. The bold pup is going to be more determined and more excited. How do I get excitement out of the bold pup? I watch him, and when the bold pup is doing something wrong, I correct it. If he doesn't listen, I correct again. Each time I correct, I have to get firmer and mean it. Let the dog figure out which is right and which is wrong. I'll notice that bold pup, when he starts to think, that's when I see the change and I'll see the puppy's mind change. I'll not see the mind work if I don't give him the chance, if I lay him down for example. If the pup is wrong, or the dog is wrong, owners use a down command and that stops the wrong but it doesn't let the mind think in the process.

Sometimes we don't think what's best for the dog. We think we know but we don't. I've worked with these dogs all my life, and the longer I work with these dogs and study them, the more they teach me. Allowing the dog to think is what I believe the answers come from. Not me making the dog do as it's told, but rather, the dog making a choice of right by working with the correction.

Some people might read this and say, "Well, my dog will not listen; he will not stop." That's simply because you didn't go through the process correctly in the first place. This isn't gong to work unless you go through the process and teach your dog to think, to listen, and to give. If you raise that pup to get him to think, I would guarantee your dog will listen, work, and do what he's told.

# Chapter 18:

# Young Dogs

Leading up to starting a young dog, I just give it freedom. A puppy is allowed to grow up as one of the dogs. The thing is, when I walk them or have them out, I don't feel that I need to play with these dogs or do anything special. I just let them be. I correct the wrongs, and in the process they learn who I am and what I am. I think the big thing is that a dog that grows up that way and knows when you are angry, knows when you are happy, knows when you are sad, knows when you are disappointed, is no different than a person. I think dogs have a lot more feeling than many, many people even give them credit for. Even myself, that is something, as I grow older and study dogs more, I see more of that in them.

For example, when I let my dogs out and they are running and carrying on and doing something that I call stupid, they get a correction. They are not made to lie down, they are not made to stop; they get a correction which gets them to think. In the process of thinking the dogs will change.

Jack getting started at a clinic in Lexington, Virginia.
*Photo by Tom Moates.*

I have a puppy now that is maybe six or seven months old, and he is a nice puppy and a good listener. When I take the dogs out, I sometimes take them while I ride my quad bike. Yesterday when I was taking him down the road I got to thinking, "you are just running and learning a bad habit. You are learning to be excited rather than running with your mind at work." I started just correcting him and having him come back and follow the bike rather than run ahead. It was just amazing for me to watch that pup change in that short time.

I never even did stop the bike and get off. I flung my hat at him and gave him a little bit of correction, and before I knew it that tail was down. When it did go up I could just say, "Max," and I would see his tail go down and his mind think. To me that is tremendous in a dog. If you can get that relationship with your dog it means that when you start to train it and it is wrong, you can talk to him and you are going to see that dog think.

I get a lot of these things watching people when I go to clinics and the way they deal with the dogs and talk to them. People are either so strict that the dogs are not allowed to do anything, or they feel they need to play with them and let them have fun. I am not saying these things are wrong. I am saying this is something that is really important. I really believe a thinking dog is a happy dog. I don't think an excited dog is a happy dog. On the other hand, I certainly don't believe a dog that is disciplined too much is happy.

I usually have from nine to 12 dogs at a time and as you well know when I let them out they are wanting to run, chase, and play. I don't say that my dogs wouldn't do that, as they get to do it now and again; however, there is a happy medium in there. This is something that really annoys me, when dogs get to running and chasing and knocking each other over and doing stupid silly stuff. To give you an example, I remember going to a clinic once, and when I approached the field a bunch of dogs were running and playing while the handlers were visiting, talking, and doing other things. Some of them were throwing Frisbees and balls and doing different things with their dogs. As I opened the gate and looked down the field I thought to myself, "that would drive me crazy if my dogs were doing that." I never said anything. I just went on down and watched and talked to people.

The next day when we went out the same kind of activities happened. When I start a clinic for the first go round I usually have the people introduce themselves and tell a little bit about themselves and their dogs. There was a dog that had quite a bit of training.

It had been to different trainers, and one of the people who had trained this dog happened to be at the clinic.

I asked, "Do you think I could send that dog for these sheep?" She said, "Yes."

I sent the dog for the sheep, and of course it went to the sheep right enough but it took me 10 minutes to catch her. The next day this dog had improved some and instead of being hyper and excited, it was beginning to think.

There was a follow up clinic to this, a two-day clinic followed by another two-day. When I went back to the second clinic, the lady who owned this dog, which had improved quiet a bit, decided to put it back in the second clinic. As I was driving down to the field, I saw the dogs running, playing, and carrying on much as they had done on the previous two days before the clinic. As I approached the field, there were three people with this same dog. They had it on a leash and it was just wagging its tail, fussing to be petted. They were trying to make it lie down and do different things with the dog, and for some reason this just annoyed me.

I said, "Bring that dog over here."

As it came over, I gave it one firm correction and that dog just went down. I did not tell it to lie down; it just hit the ground and everybody just went quiet. When the dog would start to get up I would say "hey" and it would lie back down.

The change in that dog, compared to two days previous, was just amazing. When something like that happens, naturally it makes you think. I have thought a lot about it. Why did the dog change? I think the big change was all that the correction added fear, not from what I had done as much as from the speed it was given and the tone of my voice. It was not that I hurt the dog at all, but the shock and the speed in which it happened changed the dog's mind. When that mind started to come back, I was ready to talk to it and I knew how to talk to it. I did not tell the dog to lie down; I did not make the dog do anything. I just said "hey" and the dog lay down on its own.

Within a minute or so, I bent down, took the chain off, and as the dog was going to get up I said "hey" and the dog lay down again. I said to the owner, "call your dog," and each time she called the dog I would tell it "ah, ah" and it would just wait. There was nothing I had done to make the dog do that. That dog did that on its own. Why did it do it on its own? The dog did it on its own because I allowed the dog to think.

I am even more a big believer that dogs need to think; they need to have the chance to think. It's only fair that the dog has a chance to think. To me, a dog being allowed to think for itself is much more important than a person trying to make a dog happy. If I was picking a fault in my students or people I work with, this is maybe one of the big faults: they so want to make the dog happy. Happiness comes through what the dog is thinking, not by letting it play. Why do people think that by doing that stuff to dogs that they are happy? A lot of people when they see a dog wagging its tail or jumping, running, and chasing then think the dog is happy. I don't really think it is. I don't think the mind is working right when the dog is doing that.

Allowing dogs to think is a big part of how I begin raising and preparing my dogs for training. The big difference I see with my own dogs compared to others is the change my dogs give. It is something that I really enjoy in my dogs. There are lots of different ways to train dogs, and I've trained dogs many different ways myself, but what I am trying to get through in this story are the things that fascinate me about these dogs and the things that I really feel are important. Nothing makes a dog happier than pleasing its owner. How you get that dog to please is a big part of training.

To watch dogs change like that and to gain respect for the owner and his commands are crucial. To go off the subject a little, it is the same way with the sheep or the cattle you are working. Very few people give thought to the sheep they are working. I think that is so important. If I have three sheep that are thinking, I'm going to be in heaven because, even if they are wild, if they are thinking, they can be tamed by handling the dog right in relation to them. If the sheep are just excited, crazy, not thinking, or not using their minds, then you are in trouble. By getting this dog prepared right, when you go to these sheep, you are going to find that the dog is going to change the sheep very quickly. Why is it going to change so quickly? The change in the sheep will happen because the dog is going to be thinking, he is going to be positioning himself, and he is going to find the balance point on these sheep. He is going to know how to put pressure on and how to take pressure off the sheep without being told. Often, we are not training to get the dog on to the pressure point or that balance point.

Today, it is about open flanks and backing dogs off. When the people come in and say the sheep are being wild and they are not being shepherded the way they used to be, it's because we are not allowing dogs to feel sheep or the sheep to feel the dogs. I am a big believer in that; I think sheep would change if people would change. It's not how often the sheep are handled; it is how they are herded that makes a difference.

I am sure not only me but other people find that the sheep my wife Kathy and I own are nice to work. We get the comment all the time from people that come to our trial every year, how good our sheep are. We don't do anything special to the sheep. They are treated right, the dogs treat them right, they know feel, and they know how to feel. They are not the easiest sheep to run on; they are always a challenge. I go to a lot of clinics where the sheep are either wild or they are what we call "knee knockers" that always run to your feet. They run to your feet and stay at your knees because of the way they have been handled. Whether a person has four sheep or four hundred sheep shouldn't make a difference; it is how they are handled and it all has to do with their minds.

When I say some of these things, I think a lot of people might think that my dogs are unhappy; they are always being corrected or

A dog relaxes after short work session while Jack discusses the finer points of what took place with the group at a clinic in Lexington, Virginia. *Photo by Tom Moates.*

they are always being this and that. I don't think they are unhappy at all. I think back to my own growing up quite a bit, and I think a lot of these ideas come from the way I was raised. We didn't get a lot of toys; we didn't get a lot of things to play with. We were loved and we were given everything else but we found things to play with. We found ways to make life interesting, to make life enjoyable. So how did we find that? We found that by using our minds.

So why do we need to do all of the other things we are doing today? When I look in my daughter's room and see all the toys and things she has, it just makes me shake my head and think, I never grudge them and I don't think much about them other than I think it is unnecessary. I really think we as people have caused all that. No difference between people and dogs and sheep, everything has a mind and I think it is so important that we try to GIVE whatever or whomever it is the chance to use that mind.

There is an interesting thing that I have had happen over and over when a cow would calf and something would happen to the calf. I would have to work on that cow and she would be wild and a bit crazy out of fear as I would try to get her in. Each day I would get her in and that cow would start to change. It's amazing how the wildest cow can turn into the quietest cow. I would see the change and it's from how I treated that animal.

You know you can't always just be nice to that cow, but you can't be the other way either. When the cow gives, you give. When the cow is crazy or putting pressure on, you have to hold that pressure. You have to give that cow a chance to use her mind to think. It is something that is pretty interesting to me and maybe to others it might not make much difference. The reason I am clearing up these things is because these things make a person think about training the dogs and why it is so important to give them that freedom. To me, freedom is not letting the dog run and play and do what he wants; freedom is giving the dog the opportunity to do whatever he wants but correcting the wrong when it happens. This allows the dog to start to feel some respect for himself. It is a subject I could go on and on about, and I am sure I will talk more about it as I go along.

In the early stages of training, a lot of people, myself included, were told you never take a dog to sheep without a down. It was something I have thought a lot about and it does not make sense to me. Why would you stop something before it starts? The only answer I came up with is, because of control. Long ago, if you didn't have control of your dog when you took it to sheep, you would have been in trouble. A farmer didn't want to see his sheep abused so your dog had to be controlled. When I think back on that and all the things I have been saying about raising your dog, if you raise your dog right, that control will be there...you will not need to control; you will not need to down; you will not need all of that other stuff.

In dog training I have used pretty much everything the same as everybody else. I have done different things like using long lines and chasing a dog; all these things to put stops on my dog and they all work. However, I really think that the one that works the best is when the dog gives it to you rather than you making it. When I am ready to start my young dog, it knows me. In other words, it knows how I am feeling when I go out with it. It knows if it's wrong and when I change the tone of my voice, it knows how to think. The dog doesn't need a command. It doesn't need the "stop" or "you do this" or "stay."

At many of my clinics, the first thing people do is lay the dog down, step out in front of it, and make it run around the sheep. That is, they don't make it run around the sheep, they make it run around themselves to get to the sheep.

I have changed all that. When I start my young dog, I just go in and I go to the sheep so that the dog, if he wants to chase the sheep, has that chance. If he is wrong, I correct; if he is right, I will leave him alone.

At a clinic, many of my students send their dogs to the sheep, then correct the dogs for any wrong they caused. My answer is to go to the sheep, let movement encourage the dog to chase or herd. This allows the dog to choose the right or wrong which in turn can be corrected and the dog will find its own answer. It's the same idea: if I want a dog to chase a ball, I don't make her go to chase the ball; I roll the ball so the dog will chase the movement.

When I went to my second clinic, the clinic host had a ring in a field, the ring being about 50 feet in diameter. It was built with

Jack getting to this dog's mind before stepping back and allowing freedom for the dog to do his outrun. *Photo by Tom Moates.*

snow fence. I worked the young dogs in that ring and I just fell in love with it. I have been an advocate of the ring ever since. Why is the ring so important? I think the ring is important because of the pressure points, because of the freedom. When you build a ring it has to be dog proof as well as sheep proof so that the dog, when you put pressure on to correct, has no way away from that pressure or can escape out of the ring. I want my dog to feel the pressure. So, what is pressure? Pressure is just a balance point to the dog the same as the dog is to the sheep. When you go in a ring, any movement you make is either pressure on or pressure off. That is why it is so important to know how to use a ring. The more I used it, the easier it became.

When I walk into the ring, I want to give my dog freedom to be right or wrong. Yet many people are scared to take the leash off the dog. Why are they scared to take the leash off? They are scared because they have no trust in their dogs. Why don't they trust their dogs? They didn't leave the freedom to correct the pups as they matured.

A lot of time people want to be in control of a dog so when they walk in the ring, they will lay the dog down. If you watch them, they are scared to take the leash off. When they take the leash off the dog, most of the time the dog is threatened to stay there. He is in trouble if he doesn't stay until they get in position to let that dog go. To me, that is like putting a bullet in a gun and waiting on somebody to pull the trigger. I don't want that in my dog when I start him.

I want a dog to go in, and when I take that leash off if he dives at the sheep and just goes crazy, I won't be mad at him but I will start there. I will start on that correction. I will put him back on his leash, take him back out, and when he comes in the next time, I will watch his reactions. And if I think he needs a correction, I will give him a little touch with that leash, a jerk, or something to just get him to think. Then the minute I see that dog think—and that's the secret, to be able to see him think—I will take that leash off and try it again. I will concentrate on walking in and out of the gate with that dog and getting him to think before we go.

If he is thinking the next time I walk in the gate, I might just go and kind of shoo the sheep, and if he goes I might just say the dog's name with a "hey." If he thinks and gives, there is the answer coming. That is the dog giving to you; that is not making the dog. As I do that, all I do is just let him circle there and have some fun. What I mean by having fun is to let him use his instincts.

At this point he might be kind of chasing and his tail might be up a bit, but as I am talking to that dog I would see him begin to change. I would see him trying to listen and think and watch all of these things. I always tell people, the only time you should be stepping forward to your dog in a ring or approaching your dog in a ring, is basically to correct; always be stepping off to ask. I block in the ring, I don't point in the ring. I make the wrong difficult and the right easy and the dog will follow that.

Before I know it, I will have a dog circling and giving distance. All of the sudden, I will see that dog change from the chasing dog to the eye contact—the tail dropping, the shoulders dropping down, and the natural instinct that has been bred in that dog start to come out. At that point I will try to read whether he is a strong or a mild dog, is he going to need to be backed off or brought on. Why does he need to be backed off? Normally a dog needs to be backed off to allow him to find his own feel.

I don't want to put feel in him, I want him to learn his own feel. To me, every dog has his own feel. Feel is a pressure point between the dog and the sheep. This is one of the things I think today that a lot of dogs are never given the chance to experience. Today, we make the feel; we decide the distance that dog has to be off the sheep. When we do that, if we are not right, that dog gets running either a little too far off his sheep or too close to his sheep. He is always adding pressure to the stock. So how do we find that part? We need to watch the stock; the stock will tell us.

As I go around the country, I get people saying, "well, what kind of sheep do you want? Do you want really quiet sheep for the beginner dog or do you want wild sheep for the beginner dog? Do you want this? Do you want that?"

I don't care. I want sheep, and I want to bring about a change in these sheep by using the dog so that the dog is getting the chance to change from that experience rather than me making. There are very few people who would agree with me on that, but that is just me; that is what I want.

I like a dog who knows how to circle his sheep either way, circling sheep and giving. If he comes in too tight, I'm going to back him off so that we've got an orange-shape. And we're going to try to make that orange into a pear. A lot of the time, before I start the fetch motion, I'll teach him to stop. I always back off when I ask for a stop, and move forward to correct.

Imagine a dog going around, say, at 12:00 in the ring, and I am at 6:00. I'm backing up to the side of the ring, and I say, "Aghh!" and if he gives, I give. When he goes the other way, I do the same again; I just go back and forth and back and forth until he starts to feel the sheep from behind and the pressure of the sheep starts to move him across the ring. This is the first part of the fetch beginning to form. As I'm doing that, I keep asking him to lie down, lie down, lie down.

At this point, I might go to correcting the down, instead of working on the fetch. I would move towards my dog correcting the mistake by the feel of my pressure. As soon as the dog gives any inclination to answer, I would back up, giving freedom to the dog to accept the command. He might decide just to stop, or he might just lie down; I would accept that. He doesn't have to lie down. I don't want a man-made down; I want the dog to give me a down. To me, that's important later on with my dog. There's a lot of dogs that have been made to lie down, and there's a lot of dogs trained different ways. I've trained a lot of dogs different ways myself. But nowadays I think this is the best way, and that's the reason I'm trying to give this explanation.

# Chapter 19:

# *Driving*

Starting the drive on dogs can often be difficult, yet there are some who would as soon drive as gather. As for me, I would still go for balance, feel, and gather first, as it is easier to help a dog at this stage.

When we start off by moving the stock, the dog's first move is usually to chase or herd. If he is wrong, it's easier to add pressure while he circles or fetches. In other words, it's much easier to correct and yet be in the position to see the change or read your dog's mind. As the dog changes and we allow freedom, confidence grows and our corrections, tones, and how we use them begin to show. Most of the time I like to have all this on my dog before I get into the drive. This way, when the dog is wrong, we change tone, the dog thinks, and a thinking dog comes up with his own answers.

As I start the drive, the dog starts to go up on sheep, and I like to be able to say his name or "hey" and see the dog observe or think.

If he does not, I may use the lie down, then walk up, but I will make sure it's all done in the right tone.

Remember, at this time our dog is trying and it's very important for me when a dog is trying to keep its mind free. One of my favorite sayings is, "a small try will give the big answer." During this stage, we are often looking for too much; when our dog tries and shows a slight wrong we want to correct. This correction, if used, has to be what the dog is ready to accept. Many times we look for too much and over correct rather than using caution. At this point, my dog may only be following the sheep and sometimes with little or no interest. Then is when I would give a little encouragement, a "sh-sh-sh" or "come on, come on." One has to be very careful at this point not to hurt the dog's confidence.

Many people, when starting driving, will use flanks and stops, and it works for them. For me, I want my dog to feel as he learns, as much as he feels his sheep when fetching. As the feel begins to show, then I would add the flanks and stops. Training dogs, as we all know, takes lots of time and patience. Wait for a dog, don't make him, is how I train. When teaching a young dog to drive, I want to know he feels me and I feel him. In other words, that we trust each other, so I am able to help. It may seem funny to some, but relationship to me gives many answers. It's not just getting a drive on the dog, it's getting a drive with feel and trust. When we work for each other, that is when the best answers happen.

When teaching a young dog to drive I often use a fence line to help make it easier for my dog and me. I might start with sheep in the corner, walk back from the sheep, and then send my dog, much as I would on a small outrun. As he reaches the corner and the sheep move off up the fence line I would back up and allow my dog to fetch towards me. At this point I would be looking for my dog to find the right contact and feel, as he finds that feel, then I would look for pace. As all of this develops, I move back off the fence allowing the sheep and dog to move up to where they would be parallel to me.

While keeping pace, we would move on up the fence line. If at this point the feel, pace, and contact are right I would fall back allowing the dog freedom to take the sheep on up the fence line. If a dog is on the right pressure point he should be in control of his sheep, so if they move off the fence he can give and yet hold this pressure.

The whole idea of the fence line is the dog only needs to hold the pressure on the one side and in the process keeps and builds control and feel. As the dog progresses, I would step further back allowing more freedom so as the dog not only builds confidence in me but, at the same time, feels in control, which in turn builds trust. When it's going well I'll give more freedom. If and when the dog starts going wrong, I would approach correcting until pace and feel return. I want my dog to give me this rather than I have to make it. As we progress and he can take control up most of the fence line then I would start allowing the sheep to come off the fence allowing my dog to be in full charge of both sides.

As most people who train dogs know, dogs are all different and some dogs pickup driving easily. With the easy ones, I may never have to use the fence, but find it very useful especially for keeping pace and control, which, in the end, is what I want in my dog. Driving stock for me is not about left, right, stop, walk up—in other words, having the dog make the line. It's about a dog that is in control, correcting the wrongs, and allowing the stock to find the easy way, on the feel they are getting from the dog in charge. There was an old saying that a good dog could drive sheep on the end of his nose. It's hard to find that dog anymore.

Driving is another place where I find myself in disagreement with our judging system. Today we judge lines rather than dogs being in control, with feel and pressure, coming from the correct pressure points. It's funny at trials today; we watch people walk the course to see the lines, and yet if I were judging they would be the last things I want to see. I can always remember my great friend and pal, the late J. H. Wilson, saying to me, "the day you and I, Knox, have to walk a course before we run it is the day we will quit." And to all who knew Johnny, they will remember the many great runs he had and the many great gifts he left us to think about. I feel today as we try to perfect our handling skills we take away the many talents these great dogs have to give. Far, more than trial success, the dogs' talent is what I live for!

# Chapter 20:

# Penning and Shedding

When I get questions at a clinic about penning and shedding sheep, it's usually asked, "At some point during the clinic could I work on the pen," or "Can you teach me how to shed?" It seems to me little or no thought goes into the question, "is my dog prepared or ready for the exercise?" People just want to be able to pen and shed. It's my opinion that our dogs are asked to do exercises and yet have never been prepared for the jobs they are being asked to do. Our wants are easy, but our dogs' needs are hard if we do not take the time to prepare their minds for the tasks we ask them to do.

So, what are my thoughts on when a dog is ready for the next step whether it be the pen, the shed, or for that matter any part of their training? I want my dog prepared for the step or procedure that I ask of him. I want a dog that trusts, wants to give, is willing to listen and yet, keen to try. The dog must be prepared for corrections, willing to try and accept, but also free to understand that, as I correct the wrong they get an understanding of the correction by the tone of voice that the correction is given in. For me, too many people want all the answer based on the command, but I want the answer understood between my dog and me.

When I am disappointed I want my dog to be the same; I want that dog prepared or trained that when he lets me down he knows it. He reads my disappointment and can feel from my tone how I feel because we have taken the time to prepare all of this as we go through our training process. I find that penning or shedding becomes a lot easier when our dog is prepared the correct way. For example, when my dog is wrong I want that dog, when I say his name or "Hey," to think. As he thinks, it's my responsibility to be ready to help by whatever it takes, be it corrections, encouragement or just being left alone. When my dog and I read each other the correct way, it makes life easy for both of us. Helping each other is the name of the game, if one takes the time to build it.

Let's look at penning, an exercise that tests a dog in most situations: balance, feel, power, and control. Penning is an excellent test for our dogs provided we use it the way it was meant to be, the practical way, allowing our dog contact with the sheep and correcting the mistakes. I watch penning today, where we go to the pen, the dog is laid down, we wave our stick, stamp our feet, jump up or down, the sheep go in, and we close the gate. There may be only one or two points lost and yet our dog has done nothing. For me, this is one example in our trialing where we are letting our dogs down. We play it safe, but in the process take away everything that penning should be when it comes to improving our dogs.

Today, it seems to me, sometimes when a dog has trouble at the pen, works hard, covers well, uses pressure and feel the correct way, yet he gets down-pointed for the good work he has done. We can't test weak dogs lying on their bellies. Back to training a dog for the challenge; we have to give him the sheep, correct when he's wrong, and allow him to feel and develop the right feel between him and

Jack discussing the finer points of shedding and penning with the group. *Photo by Tom Moates.*

his sheep. If he is grippy, we have to teach him how to use himself, correcting the wrong, again using tone, patience, and time. If he is weak, we have to build confidence as to how he can use what power he has. At the pen a dog who has to move to control flighty sheep, as long as he is in control and on the pressure point, is what I would want. Yet at many trials, I see dogs down-pointed for what I feel is good work. I do a lot of work with sheep on a fence or in a corner, where I can use pressure and feel to build on a dog's power. If the dog is weak, we build on confidence and teach a dog how to use what power he has.

I remember my brother-in-law having a dog, one that was purchased for a lot of money, so of course I had to go look at this dog. He was a good dog but for me lacked power, and I confessed that he was not for me. This dog would come to within eight or 10 feet of his sheep and his next move, when asked, was dive and grip. When I was back to visit three weeks later, my brother-in-law said, "come on I'll show you Ben." He took out Ben, put sheep in a corner and walked Ben up until he was touching noses with his sheep. In fact, he would get so close he would chatter his teeth, but not grip or bite. I thought he looked tremendous.

I remember asking, "how did you accomplish that?"

His answer was, "a lot of cigarettes and a ton of patience."

This was an answer I have never forgotten. Training dogs is about correcting faults, not making answers. I feel in today's trialing world we are too busy trying to make answers instead of correcting the mistake, which should give the answer.

When it comes to penning, or most of the other exercises, when things go wrong, look for the problem and go back and correct whatever is causing it. Correcting the wrong is better than making an answer.

Yes, penning sheep for me is about having your dog prepared for the job. A good friend with a top dog when we were discussing his pen told me, "if my dog cannot pen the sheep neither can I." He said, "I seldom talk to my dog at the pen." In other words, his dog was trained the right way.

On to the shed: what is the purpose of shedding sheep? It's again back to practical work. Dogs are used for shedding in many practical work situations. Each year at the end of breeding season, we had to shed the rams out of each group of ewes on the hill to bring them home. For people who don't understand, when shepherding hill sheep on a hirsel, which was one shepherd's mountain, we had what we called a cut of sheep. A cut of sheep was trained to run on its own part of the mountain. Each shepherd might have eight or ten cuts on his hill. These sheep ran in their own groups and during breeding season they were gathered each day in their own group to make it easier for rams to cover or breed the ewes. In the process, it was important that each group had the right rams for that heft or cut of sheep. If one ram had strayed from the other heft it had to be shed off and returned across the mountain to its own cut of ewes.

This was something we checked each day as part of a shepherd's work, and a dog who could shed right would make the job much more enjoyable as well as easy.

At the end of breeding season we would go to gather the rams in off the hill. As we rounded up each cut of sheep, we would shed off the rams and proceed with only the rams onto the next cut. After sorting all of our cuts, we might have a group of 20 to 25 rams that would then be taken home and put in their own enclosures. Real work was made easy with a well-trained dog.

I worked for a guy once who would not allow anyone to take lame sheep into the pens. To sort them, one had to shed the lame sheep off, then take them to a corner in the pasture to catch them and fix or doctor their feet. This could be 20 or so out of a 150 flock that we shed off. The idea behind this was to not take foot problems to the pens so as not to spread them. For me, thought went into what we did then rather than speed or ease.

Back to shedding: when I teach a young dog to shed, I prefer to have him pretty far along in his training. He knows correction, flanks, recall, tone, and all the things like that, so that when he is wrong I have them there to help the dog understand better. I teach the dog to want to shed rather than make him shed. I start off with a group of 20 or more sheep. Then I run the sheep between the dog and myself and ask him to come in. If he is struggling to come through the sheep, I step in and help make that opening. My goal at this point is for the dog to make the split or shed rather than me make it for him.

As they catch on, I find that dogs love this challenge: coming in, feeling the pressure, and learning how to hold that pressure. Sometimes, if I have a dog that is unsure I will then use a corner. I take sheep to the corner, hold them, and start off by running or letting a few go. While this happens, I keep my dog holding the sheep left in the corner. Dogs get pretty keen on holding pressure and that's one thing I want as I teach my dog to shed. I want a dog wanting to come in on the pressure, not coming into a space. The difference being, I give a dog something to do—coming in on pressure—and it's something they get keen on.

It's all preparation for me; give the dog his sheep and correct mistakes. As dogs feel this pressure they begin to like it and the more they like it, the more we have to correct. I want a dog's instinct at work as I train and not so much doing what he is told. Many dogs are trained to shed by the owner making a space, then asking the dog into that space, and then downing the dog. This, for me, is repetition training rather than feel, and it's the feel I like as I train. As the dog gets better on coming in, making his own space, and turning on the right sheep, I start refining my dog to hold the pressure without too much movement. Remember we've already taught the dog to hold the pressure, which, in shedding means the head or balance point at the head. As they progress, more movement is allowed, as long as my dog stays back, holds the pressure, and is in control. As the shed improves, the sheep numbers would get less. For me, it's all about a dog that wants to shed, not having to be made to do it. A dog that is prepared before hand so he can understand the challenge, pick up on my corrections, end up feeling good at what he is giving, in return makes me feel very good.

# Chapter 21:

# The Sheep

We talk of sheepdog trials—their ups, their downs, the good, the bad, how the sheep today were really good or how they were just wild and crazy—but seldom do we talk about why. At clinics, I try to tell the students how the sheep are, maybe, the most important part of our set up, and how, if studied, can be one of the dogs' best learning tools. Here are my thoughts and views on the sheep and where some of these thoughts have come from.

Growing up, my love for the sheep and the sheepdogs has always been my dream, one that I have followed and still today get more out of than maybe I deserve. Why? Well I guess it's the unanswered. For me, it seems that the more I feel I know about sheep, the more they prove how much I have to learn. This is not a bad thing in life as it keeps the mind and thoughts working to find these answers.

I can remember when I started as a shepherd and what it all meant for me. How I felt I knew it all and how truthfully it was

**Driving a neighbor's flock eight-and-a-half miles down a highway for a local farmer.**

all still to learn. The sheep were something I thought I knew a lot about. I had grown up around them, been around lots of shepherds, farmers, and people whom I respected, and being a young teen I thought I knew it all. However, the sheep were there to teach me how little I knew and, believe me, still are today. Yes, these sheep, that some judge as dumb, have so many answers if only we can stop and look for them.

I get so many people today, who say, "Oh, it's okay for people like you who have had the chance, the experience, the this the that."

My answer is, you have the chance, start now. Watch your sheep, think why they are acting the way they are, and try finding that answer by changing how you handle them instead of trying to make them do it your way. The sheep will adjust if one gives them the chance to use their minds.

The best example I have for that is my wife, Kathy. When she started out, a sheep was a sheep, and she had little or no experience around them. Yet, today I watch and see someone I admire—yes maybe envy a little—on how she can read sheep, and her "know how" around them. Sheep, if studied, are the best teachers we have to tell us where our dogs need to be, if we would only look

In today's modern world, we think we can use our dogs to make our sheep right rather than use our dogs to feel and correct sheep. The sheep, when corrected the right way, then given time to think, will come up with their own answers. For me, this is where sheep and dogs find respect, feel, and adjust in the correct way for each other.

When I look at sheep now, I think back to my humble beginnings. I think of the shepherds I worked with and how they used their dogs. They used them the best they could to get their work done but with little thought on how, with a little help, their dogs could have given so much more. In the process, the dogs could have helped take the fear out of the sheep and the sheep, in turn, would have given their answer by respecting the feel of the dog.

As an example, when we gather sheep, say to take them to the pens for work, our number one thought is to get those sheep from A to B, usually the fastest way we can to get on with the job. Yet, when the sheep reject the pressure, we just add more, never giving thought to why the sheep are fighting our pressure. Usually sheep fight this pressure because of fear we have instilled in them, and instead of adding more, we need to ease off and only hold that pressure. This allows our sheep to calm down and in the process gives them the chance to use their minds. As the fear leaves, sheep left to think usually will find the easy way in. In comparison, sheep forced will make the job harder.

I can remember my early years of shepherding and especially the spring when we would round up the sheep from the mountain for docking time. At this time of year, the young lambs might be from seven to ten weeks old and, of course, at this age were very dependent on their mothers. As we proceeded to gather the hill, the

**Jack's early years in Winsconsin with Craig, Glenn and Nell as they drive sheep towards the gully.**

young lambs would become miss-mothered and, one can imagine, the fear set in along with panic. This was when a shepherd needed a good dog that could stay back and hold pressure, allowing the sheep to think, settle, and re-mother a little. After they mothered-up a little it was time again to move on quietly toward the pens.

Reaching the pens was an art in itself; the sheep needed enough pressure without too much. Much as we see on our trial field, we took the sheep to the pen mouth, covered the wrongs and allowed the sheep to find and follow the opening. I have seen many mad shepherds with excited dogs have near disasters at this time, as one can imagine with 400 to 500 ewes and lambs. As the ewes and lambs started miss-mothering, lambs would break up the mountain with mothers close behind. Panic and fear set in, along with a whole day's work at the mercy of these dogs covering, trying to hold pressure, and allowing time for the dust to settle.

**Through they go with all dogs in control.**

I often think of those times and why it was happening; now my answer comes with ease; it's because they would not take time to correct the wrong. Here were the experienced shepherds who would not take the time to train and help their dogs feel and read the sheep. A dog needed to be able to stay back, cover, and allow sheep to settle and think. The shepherds knew in themselves that was what was needed but never took the time to train the dog so as sheep could understand and, in fairness, give the answer they were looking for.

One shepherd, whom I have always remembered, had this little dog named Gale. I thought Gale could have been something special but she had been taught at an early age how to catch and hold a young lamb on the hill so he could doctor it. He used to brag about her; however, when I watched her in situations such as gathering, if a lamb broke she would run, pounce, and then hold that lamb while he watched 50 or 100 others break to freedom up the mountainside and a disaster was the outcome...good memories with lots of answers if observed the correct way.

I think of things like this when I hear handlers say at trials that the only way to move these sheep is to bite. It's funny when we think of sheep, how as long as they are doing or giving the answer we want they are great, yet the minute they give us a problem, how bad or terrible the sheep are. Instead of us looking or facing this problem that we don't want to accept, we blame or criticize the sheep—instead of looking at the problem they have given us a chance to solve. Facing problems and finding answers is what sheep can give us as long as we want to learn. Wanting to win and blaming sheep will only keep making us losers.

There is so much that comes to mind when I think of sheep and how they use their minds—simple things like before coming to America, the place I shepherded on was a hill farm. The last four or five years before coming we decided to make it easier by bringing sheep into the fields for lambing. For people who don't know about hill sheep, many of these sheep had their yearly spot or place where they would go each year to give birth. The first year we brought these ewes into an enclosure or field for lambing, one could see how unhappy and uncomfortable they were. They were very unsettled, and it was amazing to watch as a ewe was approaching birth time how she would go looking for a way out to go find that favored birthplace. To the extent we almost near decided to let them go back to their hill and their freedom. Instead we stuck with it and although it caused some extra work that first year it ended up all worth it.

The following year, when lambing time came around we would have said they were ready and waiting to come in. In the years that followed, many ewes had their own spot for lambing inside the enclosure. People try to say sheep don't think and can't remember. It is still amazing for me to watch and study sheep. They have more answers and thoughts to give us if only we would look for them.

Our own sheep today never stop surprising me. When trial time comes round I would think they know; in fact, I know they know. Our ewes are very seldom worked during the year other than when dosing, shearing, or lambing time comes around. Yet at our trial people are amazed at how well they will handle. It's not how often one works their sheep or dogs; it's how one handles them when they are worked. There are so many things we could learn if only we would look at the livestock we work, what they need, and what they can give. First of all, we have to give the sheep freedom and watch. Sheep are smart, if one takes time to study them while asking the question, "Why are the sheep acting the way they are?" Look for that answer and when one finds it the sheep will have taught us the right answer.

# Chapter 22:

# Cows Versus Sheep

I get asked the question many times, "What is the difference in working sheep to cattle?"

For me it's the same thing; it's all about contact, pressure, and how to use it. Many people in the cattle world talk about biting dogs. A dog that bites creates fear much the same as the dog who, when you walk, wants to come in and nip your heels or leg. I don't know about others, but I feel very scared to walk away from a dog like this. I'm more inclined to face the dog and fight. I feel it is the same thing for a cow or a sheep. What is the difference for me? The dog who finds contact will hold that contact and show no fear until the cow gives is the one who will handle more cows much easier than the dog who runs in, bites, excites the cows, and puts them on the fight.

Handling livestock is all about taking the fear out and allowing their minds to work so the cow or sheep has a chance to think. Nine times out of ten, the animal who is held by the contact or pressure

Glen and Craig finish a job of moving some dairy cattle on a farm in Wisconsin leaving the herd calm and undisturbed this being the first time these cows had been handled by a Border Collie.

point by the dog, given time, will give. Each time that animal gives and the dog holds the pressure, provided the dog does not push, that same animal will gain respect. There is little difference in the mind of a sheep as there is in a cow; the biggest difference is size, and danger. If we use the mind correctly the body should move accordingly. We have this same mindset in our sheep dog world today, "If sheep don't want to move, dogs should be allowed to bite." I disagree 100% on this, but it's something I will get back to later.

A long time ago I was asked to go to Canada to do a cow dog clinic. It was in the Calgary area and I arrived on the Thursday to do a three-day cow dog clinic only to be told they as yet had no cattle in to work, so for the first day we would work on sheep. I remember we had a round pen set up down in the shade of a grove of trees and there were about 20 dogs. We started off as usual with participants introducing themselves and their dogs. We had a little bit of everything: cow dogs, heelers, Aussies, Border Collies, you name it and it would be surprising if we did not have it. There were also quite a few cowboys chewing, spitting, and giving their positive views on what we needed to handle cows.

I would be working a dog, who was tight and wanted to bite and I would stop and say, "See, this dog needs to be backed off; it's too aggressive and has no contact."

Their reply: "Yes, but if you've got an old cow with a calf down in the brush you need a dog that is aggressive, one that will bite, otherwise you would be there all day."

I asked, "Do you have a dog like that?"

Their answer was, "Yes, old Fido, if he goes in there then they are coming out...they might be missing an ear or part of a tail, but they were coming out!"

In fact, I listened to this story quite a lot most of the day. I worked at hand with some dogs beginning to show some positive changes, or at least so I thought. I was not sure what 75% of the participant's thoughts were. Night arrived and we shared a few beers and a few laughs, then went off to bed.

The next morning arrived and I was told they had 20 to 25 cows in the corral ready for me to work. While breakfast was being prepared I decided to walk up and see the cows. They were unbelievable, ears up, running from one end to the other—in other words, half crazy. I studied the cows for a short time then went back to the house and ate breakfast. When I was ready to start the clinic, I gathered everyone around and asked if they had seen the cows; some had, some had not.

"Well," I said, "I have seen them and for me they are looking pretty wild." In fact I do not remember the words I used but they were worse than that. I told them, "I have my old female, Jan, with me. It's been at least 6 months since she saw any cattle but I know she can work them. Before we start, I am going to take Jan in the corral and try to show you what little I can do with these wild cows."

Jan and I walked into the corral and at the sight of the dog the charge was on—cows coming to get my dog. I told Jan to walk up, and she approached the cow herd in a quiet but positive manner. As the cows approached, they started to slow down and within a minute or so we had a little dog and a bunch of cows facing each other. I gave that a minute or so, then asked Jan to walk up again. With a firm but positive eye, Jan approached, very steady and calm. As soon as a cow gave, I would ask Jan to stop there or slow down. She would hold the pressure or contact, and as they gave, Jan would quietly approach. I believe Jan may have nipped at a cow nose once or twice, but it was a controlled nip, always allowing the cattle to think. Within five to 10 minutes I could move the cows from end to end, stop them halfway, drive them across the corral, and then I called her off.

"Now," I said, "that's what little I can do with these wild cows, but I heard of some of the best cow dogs yesterday, so I am asking for some volunteers."

There were no volunteers, so I would point, "Sir, you have a dog, bring it in and let me see him."

I worked with about five different people with dogs. The dog would come in, bite and chase, but if a cow turned, the dog was out of the corral to safety. With each dog that entered, the cows got more aggressive and scary.

I said, "okay, that's enough." I explained the difference: my dog went in with courage, control, and was ready to listen instead of driving the cows wilder causing the opposite effect to happen. The cows had calmed down as Jan had carefully and quietly gone about her work taking the fear away and allowing the respect and trust to grow.

At this time I told the participants, "You all asked me to come to Canada and put on a cow dog clinic, but if you want my opinion I would take your wild untrained dogs back to the sheep ring. I'd get more control on them before trying to work cows that needed to get rid of fear rather than have more fear added. But, you paid me money to work cows, so any one who wants to work on the cows I'll be more than happy to help. Otherwise we will go back to training dogs on the sheep."

That was the end of the cattle at the clinic, I never worked a cow other than with my own dog: another learning experience. We have to prepare the dog for the task we hope to accomplish. So many people put dogs in situations they don't understand which is another reason to watch your dog if you hope to accomplish its top performance.

# Chapter 23:

# Trials and What They Mean to Me

As everyone knows, what excites some does not matter as much to others. We all know, trials bring out various opinions. Handlers all go out to try to win; however, there is a big variation in how. For some it's a serious deal, others it's a try, and for some it's "win at any cost" whether it's done the right way or the wrong way. After many years of following the sport, spectating, and competing, I thought I should write a chapter on my feelings about trialing; what I think from the past, the present, and what I think the future holds.

For me, trialing started way back in 1968 when I ran in my first trial. Before this, I had followed the sport and attended many trials and, looking back, feel that I enjoyed the watching just as much as the competing. It's when I look back I wonder, what is happening to this special sport? Why the feeling, the desires, the "can't wait for the next one" is declining for me? Sometimes I feel that when we have something that's good and we try to make it better, we fail.

**Jack and Jim preparing to pen at Soldier Hollow.** *Photo by Anita Pratt.*

Trialing is a sport that was started to find dogs that could handle sheep with feel, power, and control, yet give the animals freedom to respect. Along with this great dog, it gave the handlers the right to train, breed, and select from the best. When I first went to trials, the sheep were treated with respect. The first thing I learned about was the sheep. To treat sheep with respect we have to teach them. For sheep to respect our dogs, we have to allow them to feel. This is a big change in our trialing world today. It's more about placing our dogs to make sheep right, rather than to feel the pressure point and balance. One does not make things right, but if we correct our wrongs the rights will follow.

I'll watch young dogs feel their way to find the answers—the way a certain young dog on contact needs little or no movement to be in full control of the animal it is handling. Yet we, instead of watching this, want to be in control and in many cases take away the very thing we need to keep if we want our dogs and stock to be better and gain respect for each other. So how does this relate to trials? I feel the answer is simple, we are allowing the winning to overtake the correct way.

It's not always the winner who is right, but in lots of cases he or she gets the prize. I am a little different from most, but I have always been guilty of being sorry for the loser rather than happy for the winner. Not that I would ever take away or feel bad about the winner, it's just something in me that makes me feel it's the ones who lose that need the encouragement and help. I often think on an answer Kathy gave during a clinic when the discussion came up on her taking second at the National Championship. As everyone was saying, "Well, you should have won it."

She paused for a second or so then said, "Have you ever thought about what's wrong with being second?"

This is an attitude we all need to think of and share, follow, and show what this great sport is all about. I watched part of the British Open Golf Championship and was amazed as a top player made a poor shot, got mad and broke the golf club. I also watched The World Soccer Championship to see a man bite another. It makes me wonder what sport is all about anymore.

We, as handlers, have the same opportunity to show and display our dogs to the public in a sportsman like manner, with the will to win being controlled and conducted in a way that we will all be proud to be part of. Instead, we are cheating our sport by trying to win the easy way, even if we know it's wrong. I've watched handlers use themselves instead of their dogs to avoid losing points. In my opinion, when we are at the handler's stake, if we move away, we make it easier for the dog, when the answer is we should be moving the sheep around our feet. The stake is for the handler to stand at. Think how much easier this would make it for the judge, and also how it would allow the judge to see the dog with the right feel, power, and contact.

Another example is the pen, where in many cases weak dogs are made to lie down, while the handler proceeds to move, jump, and swing their crook in an endeavor to pen the sheep. Looking at the shed, many times handlers will not use the dog to avoid a grip. The above are all examples of cheating our system. In my opinion, the difference today in running dogs when compared to the past is how we behave as handlers. Today, handlers will do what it takes to win, whereas long ago the handler's pride played a far bigger place in the sheepdog trials.

I can always remember the late John Gilchrest telling me, "If you cannot do it the right way, you have no right to be out there."

I still think of those handlers today; of how proud they were of their dogs and how the correct way was the only way. Looking back on the past makes me think of the present and what we need to do to help the dog and the sheep, which supply the sport. I am a big believer in looking at our dogs for answers, rather than at the people. When the dog is correct, if it's handled right, it gives the positive answer. If the dog is wrong and corrected the right way, a lesson will have been learned. It's when we correct our wrong that things improve, not by making excuses, cheating, changing or adding rules that make the difference.

It's my own opinion that people from the past set up the rules to help the dogs, and in the process help themselves, to understand. Today we want to change rules to make answers instead of correcting ourselves, which if done correctly will give us answers. I get irritated at people today who want to have a 600 to 800 yard outrun and yet complain of the 80F to 90F degree heat. It's not how far your dog runs out that matters; it's the way in which the dogs conduct and control themselves in the process. I have had many dogs who could go out double that distance on the hill, but that did not mean they were quality dogs. Sheep dog trials should be about talented dogs that have and show that special extra. It's about feel, balance, and how they get there that matters. We are too much into trying to make things more difficult and yet when we fail want to make excuses.

I heard of a trial with a 700 yard outrun which dogs were achieving, yet 70 percent or more only made it to the handlers' feet, leaving the drives, the pen, and shed uncompleted. Maybe I am wrong, but for me this is not the way trialing is going to grow. The future lies in our hands; it's in what we need not what we want. Judging can play a major role. Let's have more outruns where the dog can see the sheep. Let's judge the dog on the way he starts the outrun. If the dog is tight and adjusts himself, leave it alone. If the dog needs help, deduct points according to how much help he needs—if he adjusts right and lands at the top taking pressure off his sheep and approaches his lift with the sheep settling to him, rather than having sheep held or trapped until he gets there. Let's judge the outrun on the dog that thinks, feels, corrects, and gives—in other words, gets behind his sheep with feel, slowing down or stopping, so as to prepare for a correct lift. The lift should be smooth and even, lifting the sheep with ease and if possible keeping contact and feel of the sheep for the fetch ahead.

For me, today, fetches and drives are based too much on lines. A fetch should be left to the dog, with the handler helping out when needed, and the judges deducting on what they see wrong. An example would be sheep going off line—but my idea of the line is different than most. Most judges want a dog to move the sheep on as straight a line as possible, but sheep don't move in a straight line. I look for a dog to move the sheep on a line that is more of a "roadway" about the width of the gap between the fetch gates. I want the dog to have control with his sheep relaxed and moving at the right pace. The drive is the same way. If sheep are weaving on the drive, is the handler causing it or the dog? Is it that the dog doesn't have the right contact? These are all things that, as judges, we may feel different about. When it comes to the pen, as I said earlier, it has to be a combination of handler and dog, with, for me, the dog showing his authority and feel over his challenge.

The shed is a place where a dog can be challenged in many different ways—his balance, control, feel, and power—but only if he is left to show them. Setting sheep up for the shed is as important as the shed itself. I see handlers set sheep up, step in, make a hole, then cry the dog in. This takes away all the challenges I have already given. A person cannot judge a dog's balance, feel, and power, if a handler is allowed to do the dog's work.

Hopefully, these are things we can talk about, think about, discuss, and make for improvement. For me, the improvement of trials means correcting our mistakes—not looking for what we want, instead looking for what we need. Let's look for answers rather than make excuses. Success comes from working with each other.

# Chapter 24:

## Views On Judging

Judging is always a touchy subject to discuss, write about, or talk about, as it seems we all have our own opinions. These are some of my thoughts, right or wrong. One thing I hear all the time is, "We need a new rule for this or that." It's not a new rule we need, we just need to be ready to accept the decisions the judges make. Should a judge keep making wrong decisions, he will ultimately eliminate himself from being asked to judge other trials. I feel there is much more that goes into good judging than any rule can ever add. Judging, from my point of view, is about the control the dog has on the sheep—the feel, balance, and contact, it has—and yet, always holding a position that, with a slight movement which can give freedom or hold pressure. Some of this may be hard for people to understand, but I will explain my views and why I believe the way I do.

I believe we have allowed sheepdog trials to become more of an obstacle course, judging lines, hitting panels, penning, and shedding anyway we can, rather than running the course the way it was meant to be done. Sheepdog trials used to be a sport filled with pride and respect plus stockmanship being shown for the way sheep were handled. In other words, if you don't want to show that your dog can control, handle, and take sheep around the course in the manner which it was set up to be, then you should not be out there. It's sad for me today to listen to how everything else is wrong: the setting of the sheep, the course, the judge, the list is never-ending. When really the real wrong is in ourselves. We need to take a hard look at ourselves and I believe we will come up with some very interesting answers. It's all about winning nowadays, not how we win. We just do it in whatever way makes a win. The pride, the art, the grace in how it's done is gone.

When I think back on the art of running a dog, how I was taught still makes lots of sense. The pear-shaped outrun and what is meant by it was developed for a purpose. Sheep, if set right, get a chance to settle at the top of the field, and will most of the time feel or see the dog leave the handler's feet at the bottom. If the dog is correct, he or she will make its way on the outrun. At this point, the dog should be reading the sheep, thinking, giving, and making that pear shape so as not to disturb the sheep on the way out, with the widest point being at 3:00 or 9:00 o'clock. The dog then should start to make the arc on the top end of the pear. If we allow our dogs to feel the sheep better as they run out, our sheep, in return, would be able to read the dog. But now we send our dogs so wide they are completely out of contact with the sheep and upon arrival only add fear to our sheep rather than take it away. This is one of the reasons why we want our sheep held at the top end until the dog arrives.

I can remember when I was taught to set sheep. We were told to release the pressure as the dog passed 3:00 or 9:00 o'clock on the outrun, giving freedom to sheep and dog to find and feel each other.

If one looks at this and thinks of the judge's job, how much easier it is to judge a dog on contact, a dog whose reaction either settles or disturbs sheep, it tells where points need to come off without the rule.

The lift begins when the outrun is complete. As the dog makes contact, it should be reading the sheep. If the dog is wrong, it's up to us as handlers to step in and help. A dog who is right on the outrun has the chance to stop, slow down, or put himself in the best position, one where he feels the sheep and gives the sheep the best chance to accept the dog. At this point, the dog should move or ease onto the sheep, making the contact without adding fear or panic. I feel the lift is a very short yet vital element in one's run. The lift is worth a lot of points, but well earned when done right. I always remember Jock Richardson telling me, "Jack, if your dog makes the right contact when they get their sheep, it's up to you as a handler to keep it." I have thought on that statement many times.

Once the sheep have moved off the lift the fetch is in progress. Again the dog must be in contact and fetching the sheep with control, which is more important to me than lines and gates. If the contact and feel is right, the chances are the rest will take care of itself. As the fetch ends, we turn the post and start our drive, another sticky point for me. So many people tell others to move away from the post and make it easier for the dog. As I shared earlier, I feel the post is where we stand until we are ready to proceed to the pen. We are supposed to turn the sheep around our feet, not the post. If sheep are hard to make that turn, it's up to us as handlers to make a wider turn and to leave it up to the judge to take care of the points.

On to the drive, which again is much the same as the fetch. The dog should be in control, taking sheep up and across our drive course. I always remember the late Johnny Wilson telling me, "Get them lined up then take them." He said sheep like when your dog is in control.

In regards to the pen, there is as much to lining your sheep up when coming to the pen as there is in penning. Sheep who are feeling the dog right will answer easier. The same with the shed. We need to allow our dogs to make the shed. We, as handlers, take away from our dogs the ability to handle situations because of the fear we have or lack of trust we have in our dogs. Handlers are the ones who make it hard for the judge because they do things the easy way, knowing that it's not the right way.

Trialing is a sport which is very hard to make even for every handler, but it's a sport that, if and when we try to do it the way it was meant to be, it can be rewarding to all. You will not always get the breaks or the right sheep, but when you try to do it the way it's meant to be done the satisfaction will come with it.

A statement made to me from a good friend after a disappointing result follows. I said, "Well, I thought you had it."

The reply was, "It all works out; I have gotten the result at times when I should not have."

This is something we all need to dwell on and think about. Sheepdog trialing is a sport that is hard to set up so it is fair for everyone. I think we, as handlers, need to try harder to accept that and keep looking at what makes the quality of the dog better. As quality improves, we will all get answers and our sport will take care of itself.

I mentioned earlier how some of this may be hard for people to understand and hopefully through some of my thoughts the message I try to pass on is clearer. It is feel, balance, and the right contact that give our sheep confidence in the dog, which in itself makes sheep easier to handle. When sheep are handled the correct way it makes judging much easier, as we can see the faults in dogs and handlers. Not only does it make the judge's job easier, it takes fear out of the sheep. It opens up the door for the better dogs and gives us the chance to show how good or bad our dogs really are when put in the pressure position. We are inclined in sheepdog trials to do what it takes to win, but let's not forget the main part in our sport. First, the sheep—without them there would be no trials—and of course our dogs. We are guilty of stepping in and making things easier for the dog, taking away any unnecessary risks, all for the purpose of winning, but in the process, taking away the chance of the quality dog to show his or herself. Winning a dog trial with a poor dog does not make that dog any better two days later. It's up to our judging system to take care of this if we want our dogs to improve and go on. Quality is the answer to success, not winning.

# Chapter 25:

## How Each Dog Can Be Your Teacher

Over the years, as I watch dogs, study people and look at livestock, I find the answers. This morning as I was watching my dogs do their early morning routine, getting out of the kennel, relieving themselves, sniffing and thinking, it got me to thinking about what is it about these dogs that intrigues me, fascinates me, and in all, makes me want to know them better. The more I thought, the more answers kept coming to me, so I decided this might be another chapter to add and let folks know me and what I am all about. Dogs are my teachers and I only wish I could put on paper a small part of what they have done, given, and taught me about life in general. I know I talk a lot about winning and how, for me, it means a lot, but it is a far cry from what these dogs are all about and maybe the lesser part in all they have to give and teach us. It's the wrong that teaches me the most whereas most winners should not be showing us too much wrong. Life today is all about winning, being the best, but for me it's about getting better, reaching to find new goals, leaving room for us all to advance. There is so much room for all of us if only we use it. Throughout this chapter I will try to give my ideas and my thoughts about how dogs today are teaching me more and more. Why? I think it's because I am more ready to watch, see, think on what they are showing, and in their own way trying to tell me. Before, I was too busy training or trying to make my dog do what I wanted, never taking time or giving thought to why it was not working. I was too convinced, in my mind, that I was right never taking time to study my dogs as to what they were thinking. It's a simple answer when we let it work. Help the dogs with their minds and as the answer comes, the reward is so much better and the respect gained between dog and handler usually amazing. As an example, I would go through my own dogs that I own at present and try to give some ideas on what I look for from them and what they give.

I watched two young dogs, five or six months old, released from their kennels. Their first move was to run, chase, play, and as far as I was concerned, I was not even in the picture. For me, this is teaching a young dog to be wrong and just another thing that will eventually have to be corrected. But in many people's eyes, this is just fun; it's allowing a young dog to grow up and gain confidence. For me, it's teaching the young dog not to care. This one fault leads to another as the correction list keeps growing.

Look at this from the human side. Say my child is being naughty, talking out of turn, speaking to adults in a manner with no respect, but we say he is "just a child," one that is yelling and screaming with no respect for others. Well, that is completely wrong in my book. I was brought up to respect adults, to speak when spoken to, and certainly not to be screaming or yelling when in company. That is no different from the young dogs I have just mentioned. Life amazes me sometimes. On a recent trip home I changed planes in Denver Airport. A mother and young child who was maybe five or six years

Jack explains his point to the crowd at a clinic in Lexington, Virginia.
*Photo by Tom Moates.*

old, sat in the seat ahead of me. As we prepared to leave we were asked to fasten our seat belts. All heck broke loose as this young child screamed, yelled, and kicked as the mother and attendant did their best to try to encourage the child to fasten the seat belt. Eventually, the pilot came back and gave it a try, but with no success. We sat there for at least 45 minutes, and finally through much persuasion the belt was put on and our journey continued. This is a prime example, of correction versus praise. In my up bringing there is no way I would have been allowed near a plane or people if I could not behave or act in an appropriate manner. I watch this and think of my dogs, and I say to myself it's the same thing.

I have just purchased a young dog, nine months or so, named Nip. Nip came from Allison Jarrard and is out of her Mist and Shep. I have done little or no training on this dog but rather have given freedom for him and me to get to know each other. He is taken out with the other dogs. Sometimes I will take him along with others to bring the ewes and lambs up at night. In the process, Nip can get quite full of himself, keen and although sometimes wrong, bearable. Right now we are going through a real hot spell, with high humidity, which of course, is hard on the sheep. Last night as I brought the sheep in Nip decided to over compensate and in the process caught me wrong. I stopped what I was doing, called Nip off in a tone by which he knew, he was in trouble. I put him on a short line and basically told him, "Hi buddy, when I speak you listen", nothing big, but enough for Nip to get the message. As I walked up to the barn, I left Nip with short line dragging and could see a very slight change. I put the sheep and dogs in for the night and went for my nightcap. The next morning, I went out and decided to take Nip and Coach to put the sheep out. The change in Nip was unbelievable, with the relationship between Nip and myself just blossoming; small change, positive answer.

My next dog is Dan who is homebred out of Kathy's Clint and Peg, He is eight months old and just keen to start. Dan, when taken to sheep just wants to dive and often at times will take a little poke. But as I watch him, I feel he needs left alone to sort some of it out by himself. Again, if I watch and search, Dan will tell me what our next move should be.

My third young dog, Bill, is the same age as Dan. As a pup, Bill was just something else. He had a great nature and was easy to be around. As he is maturing, he is becoming a little excitable. I feel some of this is coming from being around the other dogs. Bill will be interesting for me because of his personality and behavior as a pup compared to how he is reacting now. Again, I will study Bill, giving freedom to find wrong and right. It's my gut feeling that this dog will come back to the laid back type he was as a pup. Bill is already changing himself on sheep. The coolness is beginning to show more, which in itself is an answer for me.

Ettrick Craig is my next dog; he is out of Kathy's Clint and her Peg. He is one who shows good potential but for me if anything he is a little too careful. He's a good outrunner with nice pace and wants to listen. He is 20 months and is ready for more work. Many people would have this dog further along, but, I am prepared to wait. Why? Because I feel Craig needs time to find himself and when he does, his answers will come easy. I feel by the end of the year that this dog can be something special.

My next dog is a very interesting one; Brinn is out of Joe Haynes' Kealey and Michael Gallagher's Cap. She shows lots of brilliance most times but has places that bother me. Again, I am allowing time and so far I am pleased to watch her progress.

She is a small, classy bitch. She can, at times, hang up on the outrun but given time I feel she might correct herself. She can be inclined to dive under pressure but again is getting better and I feel if I'll wait I will have a better dog. For me sometimes dogs need time, something we, as people, do not want to wait for.

My last two dogs are Coach and Nap. Coach is my nursery dog. He's two and a half years old. He's out of Kate Harlan's Lucy put to Allison Jarrard's Rob. He is, in my opinion, one of the better dogs I have owned. He has a great disposition, is laid back with good feel and power. Coach has most of what I look for in a good dog. Ettrick Nap is out of Larry Birch's Dot and Ettrick Roy. Nap, on the other hand, is a little more excitable than Coach. He is a dog who wants to please and is a great outfield worker who basically trained himself. He is a dog always willing and ready to give his all. A little more eye than I would want, but a dog like Nap is a keeper. Nap is a dog, who when I started him I thought would never suit me, and yet, given time and understanding, Nap has taught me much more than I could ever have learned on my own.

Nap and Coach are two dogs whom I have great pride in. They might never reach the greatness that I feel their potential shows, but they will take a guy like me on that journey which has brought nothing other than fun, success, and a lifetime of dreams.

# Chapter 26:

# Looking for an Answer

It's a far cry from dogs, but interesting to me is how people one has never met can put such a positive message in our lives. I have been lucky to have some of these special people drift into my life and leave a positive stamp. One of these men was the late Ray Hunt, a legendary horseman who was to change horse training and thoughts on it forever. I have been told by people who knew Ray well that he wanted to meet me; for me, a meeting which would have meant so much more to my life of miracles.

I was up in Canada putting on a clinic for a friend, Jack Ragier. It was a three-day clinic and as usual, had participants and observers. Among the ones who observed was a gentleman who I had never met, but one who stood out in the crowd because of the way he presented himself: well dressed and seemed to keep much to himself. I noticed each day how he would be up at the top in the auditorium very much on his own. I don't remember him asking any questions or talking to him until the clinic ended. At the end of the clinic the gentleman approached me and said, "Mr. Knox, I want to thank you for your clinic, but most of all I want to tell you why I came to it. Jack Ragier, the man who put the clinic on, and I are very good friends and we train and work horses together. Mr. Ragier told me that I had to come watch this guy: 'He is a Ray Hunt with a dog.'"

Unknown to me, I must have had a blank look on my face because he asked, "You don't know who Ray Hunt is?"

I said, "Sorry, I don't."

He began to explain about Ray and how he could take a wild horse and in a short time not only lead him but have the horse like him. This of course impressed me right away. He then added, "I came to the clinic to stay for five minutes. Instead, I have been here for three days and I have enjoyed every minute, and you are a Ray Hunt with a dog."

This may be the best compliment I have ever received, and of course a great lead into knowing more about Ray. The more I have learned the more respect I have gained for the man; the thoughts, the feelings, the meaning I received from someone I never met are priceless.

Through all of this I heard of the Master Tom Dorrance, another I only know by name but feel like he was a close friend. Although I never met Tom, I did meet his brother, Bill, a memory I cherish. He came to a clinic I put on in Salinas, California; if I could have stopped the clinic I would have for there was a source of information I wanted to grab and save. I am so thankful to meet people of this caliber and learn and open up doors for new ways, new ideas, and yet many who come to a clinic can't see or feel these benefits. So many believe one has to work a dog to get an answer when, really, the answer comes by knowing how to work it. It's like a judging clinic; people believe that working and judging dogs is better than learning why points should be deducted.

Jack with Sandy, a three-year-old welsh pony that he rode while shepherding in Gilmansleuch.

Getting back to the story on Ray, it's unbelievable the people I have met, the stories I have heard, and how, for me, these discussions, conversation, and stories can mean as much or sometimes more, than working or helping others work their dogs. Yet many folks have trouble trying to feel the benefits of easy answers. Why? Because in our minds we feel we bring our dogs and ourselves there to benefit from working with the clinician, where I feel a change in the way we use that mind can be such a positive answer if only we would accept. A mind willing to seek and accept is the one that gains, not the one who thinks what it wants and is not willing to allow the mind to open and look for what it needs. Working with people and their dogs has taught me so much about what we need, yet there are so many who still feel what they want is better. It still amazes me why so many people feel they can gain more from a private lesson rather than a two or three-day clinic—that's an hour lesson compared to two or three days of clinic. For example, many people feel that watching beginning handlers and their dogs is a waste of time. Yet to me it is still where many of my answers start to develop. No time during a clinic is a waste provided you are willing to watch, listen, keep the right, and release the wrong. We can gain answers if we are willing to accept.

The benefits of knowing of people like Ray Hunt and Tom and Bill Dorrance is, it opens up my mind and, if used the correct way, gives new answers rather than repetition which stays the same. So many people want to compete so badly instead of watching their dog get better that they miss the point. After hearing about Ray, Kathy and I kept looking for some type of article or writing about him, and while on our way home from out west we found an article in Western Horseman magazine. I can hear Kathy read this as I drove down the highway. She said listen to this, then read, "When one rides on his horse and wants to stop, he pulls on the reins, the horse stops, but no release."

I shook my head and thought of dogs on leash—same thing, no freedom after the correction. It's like we hold on to keep our dogs from being wrong again when we should be giving freedom to let our dogs find their answers. When we are scared of the wrong, we take away the chance to correct. The things I have gained from people like Ray, Tom, Bill, people I hardly know, is more than I could ever tell. It's like people who come to me for help; they teach more than they could ever believe because they make me think. I don't know all the answers, but when I think, every answer is a possibility.

Stories that are told, as well, can be tremendous learning tools. Conversations when we talk of people, friends, of wrong things that happen, all can be sometimes more rewarding provided one thinks about them every bit as much or sometimes more than about working or training one's dog. An example of this happened to me quite a few years ago. I was doing a clinic that I have put on yearly in Wisconsin. A friend came by to watch a little which he had done most years I had been there. This friend, again a horse person, had won a national roping championship, and during our conversation he told me how he had built an indoor arena and invited me up to see it. My father-in-law and I took time to go visit and see Jim's building. As we sat in the arena that night chatting about dogs and horses, he asked how much I knew about roping. My answer was, "I know very little about horses and far less about roping." So then he continued telling me about ropers and how during their roping season their horses will sour so they lease another. Some may rope off four or five different horses during the season. As I listened to all this I must have looked puzzled. But then he said the year he won the Championship he went to 160 rodeos and roped off the same horse.

As I pondered who this guy was, he continued, "Do you know why ?"

Of course, I said, "No."

Then he said, "Because I never trained him." He said, "The only time my horse was touched was if he did wrong, then I would work a little on the wrong."

This for me was a huge answer, one that later I gave much time and thought to. This was a tremendous answer that was gained out of that story. I can remember telling my great friend, the late Johnny Wilson, this story. All who knew Johnny could tell what a brilliant handler, trainer he was. He needed no help, but I can remember a year or so later sitting in his house one night having a beer and of course talking sheep and dogs, when Johnny turned to me and out of the blue said, "Knox, you remember the story you told me about the roper?"

I said, "Yes."

Johnny said, "You know, I got miles out of that story."

So, as we sat drinking our beer, we each discussed the great details we took from the roper's story.

Another story which meant so much for me was one I was told by a participant as I conducted another clinic in California. This dear lady had come to my clinics before and she said, "I have a story to tell you, Jack; I know you will get a lot out of it."

It was a Tom Dorrance story. She explained where her house was on this big plateau and as you looked down from it there was a big meadow. This night she had friends and neighbors over, and they were out on the lawn in the yard where she served hors d'ouvres and drinks as they sat around visiting. As she was talking to Tom Dorrance he looked out in the meadow and said, "That's a good-looking horse down there."

The lady replied, "He is such a great horse but is hard to catch."

Tom listened to the story, and they sat and chatted some more. Then Tom moved over to the edge of the yard and looked at this horse down in the meadow. As the horse started to notice Tom, he then sat down. The horse stared for a little, then went back to grazing. It was then that Tom reached over and found a small pebble or rock and all of a sudden tossed it down into the meadow. As the rock hit the ground it startled the horse; Tom sat and watched the horse's reactions.

First he showed a little fear, but then he got inquisitive, as he sniffed, pawed, and made his way to the rock; many different types of emotions went through the horse's mind. As the horse figured it out he finally was satisfied and went back to grazing. At this point, Tom got up, wandered on down into the meadow until again the horse saw movement. At this point, Tom sat down. The horse started the same behaviors as he had done when the rock landed; fear, then inquisitive, finally getting brave enough to explore, as the horse gradually made his way to Tom and felt comfortable.

Tom raised his hand and rubbed the horse with comfort. As the horse became comfortable, Tom finally got up and returned back to the party with the horse following Tom all the way. And my friend said the amazing thing was that horse was never again hard to catch. Again for me, only a story, but if read and thought of in the right way it contains huge answers that we can take away and use, as we train our dogs.

# Chapter 27:

## Putting Together Training

Summing up my training method comes naturally as it is based on the same principle as living my own life: freedom to be right or wrong. When one is right, accepting is easy. When wrong, we don't like to accept it, yet as soon as we do it makes correction much easier.

My training has a lot to do with correcting the wrong. In raising my pups, I believe it's real important to teach them how to accept that correction the easy way. When I raise my puppies I try to leave freedom of choice; they can play, they can have fun, in other words they can do what they want, but when they are wrong or doing something I don't like I correct. How I correct depends on how I need to. Say the pup is chewing on something. I might say, "Hey what are you doing?" If he ignores, I change my tone. Say he continues, then I would go correct. How I would correct depends on how I need to. It's all just common sense, but for some reason, at times we do not want to use that, but rather be told how to. Many

Jack sets a young dog up to cover sheep in a difficult position on the side of the ring. Teaching the dog to give and find her real pressure point to pull sheep of the fence. *Photo by Tom Moates.*

people are afraid to be wrong and in trying to prevent, keep making more wrongs. My advice to that is, do not be afraid to be wrong and if you are, accept it. When we accept and then correct, this makes an easy answer.

Training a puppy has nothing to do with control; it's more about allowing freedom for the pup's mind to mature. Correct when wrong; leave alone if right. Why do we praise when the pup is right? Myself, I doubt he needs it and if praised will take away from what he just accomplished. Praise is something we all want, but don't need. A mind changes the second we hear praise. It makes us feel we are good. Respect, on the other hand, comes from correcting our wrongs and in the process gaining the feeling of getting better. For me, it's much better to feel the right myself than be told. Don't get me wrong, there is nothing wrong with loving your pup; tell him he is good, just don't over do it. Make sure you leave room for his mind to think for itself. I work a lot on tone of voice; it's not what you say as much as how you say it. I feel it leaves the pup choices and when right I may just change my tone enough for them to hear and feel it. As the pup matures, I look for respect. By this, I mean if I say something I expect my pup or young dog to think. If he is thinking or acknowledging, then the answer should be forthcoming.

When we expose the young dog to stock, I prefer a small area where stock cannot run too far; this takes away from the chase. I start out by moving the stock, which in turn should light up the young dog's interest as it makes a move. If it's calm and controlled I accept; if they go to dive or chase, I speak or correct. This is a big part where the tone we have taught our puppy or young dog comes into play. If we have taught him properly, when we correct, the mind should work, and as they pause or think we must be ready to help either by stronger tone or by body movement. Most young dogs when released to sheep tend to want to chase or some can be afraid. If they show fear, I keep moving sheep and encourage. If they chase, I move towards them using tone and body movement.

Be patient at this point, remember this young dog is trying to find answers, and don't try to make them for him. Just wait, give time, keep trying, and leave the mind to sort it out. I am astounded how people want positive answers. Remember, this is all new for your dog.

It's very important at this time to be patient, relaxed, and leave time for your dog to figure it out. This is why, with a young dog starting out, I want to work only for a short period of time. It amazes me still to watch a young dog who can be completely confused and hyper the one day, be worked for possibly 4-5 minutes and yet, that same dog come out the next day picking up a billion answers. My experience is, if we wait on the dogs and give them time to figure out their wrongs, they will come up with a far more solid answer. I used to be one who wanted quick answers and as a result tried to make it easier for my dog, by using my mind instead of allowing my dog to use his. In other words, I would move into a position to help make a right rather than allow my dog to be wrong, which I believe now takes away the chance to correct. Dogs have taught me if you correct their wrongs rather than make their rights, the answers they get are far more positive.

As we start our dog circling, he may put too much pressure on the sheep, which gets them excited or hyper. I would step in and correct making it hard for the dog and as he opened, immediately take pressure off. It's the release of the pressure or correction that feeds the dog its own answer. I have changed, rather than blocked or pushed—I tend to allow the dog to have the sheep and approach when wrong. It's important to wait until the dog is wrong, not move to make him right. Start out with body pressure, and as the dog shows change or thinks, take pressure off. It's not the pressure as much as the release of pressure, so your timing and feel are very important. I like to feel as this training process improves, I can lean away from the dog or lift a hand, nod my head and at the same time talk to him. It's important, too, at this time not to put pressure on, but rather take pressure off, allowing the dog to feel the answer rather than try to make it.

As the dog starts to read me, he will start to give and as he gives he feels the control and finds his answer. This, to me, is a dog finding its own answer by correcting its own mistakes. I try to make sure on all I have done so far that my dog is willing to give when asked. It's very important when he doesn't; with a sharp tone one should see the dog's mind change. If the dog is thinking, with a little help the dog should find the answer. What is important for me at this time is that the dog is happy and keen to try. Should the dog struggle at any point, you should make it easier by going backwards in your training; going back to basics usually makes the job easy. By now the dog should understand how to give to body pressure and how the tone of the command or correction has meaning. It's those little things that make the big answers come easy.

When it comes to the outrun, I start by circling my dog, stop it, call it off, and gradually start making that circle into a pear. In the past, I would step out in front of my dog to make him cast or go out. Although this system works and makes them give, the pressure also adds tension plus hyperness with the result of tightening it up on

**This dog is too tight on the sheep as Jack signals to him to open up.**
*Photo by Tom Moates.*

top instead of giving. Now, when I send a dog, I try to move off him allowing him the sheep. Should he go straight or tight, I correct. First vocally, and if the dog does not respond I go straight towards the wrong using a harsh or deeper tone which usually by now should be effective, provided we have done our homework. As soon as I see my dog think or react, I release my body pressure and talk to relax my dog. It's important at this time to be patient and let the dog have time to figure it out. In other words, wait on the dog. Remember, we should have done a lot ahead of this to help this dog understand the basics. Correct preparation at this time makes it easier for the dog. As the dog catches on, give him time to build confidence in himself. As the confidence grows, so will the dog's feel for his sheep. As this improves we should keep lengthening the outrun. Say he takes a negative turn or struggles, shorten the outrun and bring back his confidence.

There are fewer dogs today, in my opinion, that feel sheep on their outrun. Why? Because we shape and don't allow them to. My feeling is if the dog is not allowed to feel the sheep, how are the sheep supposed to feel our dog? I can remember old timers talk and laugh about half moon outruns. I never hear of that anymore.

People today think if a dog lands right without disturbing sheep that is okay. Not for me, especially if he goes out of contact to get there. Shedding, penning, side commands, and opening flanks are covered in other chapters in this book. This is just a guide in putting my method together and, as you can see, it's all about correcting wrongs, with no plans or method to make a right. I am a true believer that if you want sheep to trust your dog, we have to let them feel it, and as they feel, we adjust the pressure and take away fear. In the process, this gives confidence to our dogs, who, by feel, take fear out of our sheep making it easier for them to understand.

# Chapter 28:

# What's Right for Our Dogs

When I first started out in the dogs my interest was more about quality, what I liked about a certain dog. What was the attraction? Why did it give me the push to try to own or get my dogs to reach that level? There was something at that time I gave very little thought to but that was the interest which pushed me and led me to where I am today.

So what is the difference today? The only difference is that I think about "why?" and the answers that keep coming. There are so many things about these dogs that I will never know, but the older I get the more I think, and the more positive these answers become. I thought it might be interesting to tell and point out my feelings and ideas on the things we can all do to give back to these dogs for what they have given to us.

Jack giving a correction as the dog tries to harass the sheep at a clinic
Notice Jack, as the dog gives, releasing the pressure.
*Photo by Tom Moates.*

To start off, I want to explain that back then, I knew little about trials. I had heard of them, but as far as interest and knowing what they were about, for me it was very little. This is the time when I would buy a dog for seven or eight pounds and put some training on him and maybe sell him for 10 or 12 pounds. I used to do a lot of that, and much of my training at that time was trial and error. I did what my brother did, or what I heard someone else had tried. These were all unregistered dogs. The registered ones I had heard of, but back then many of the shepherds had the opinion that the registered dogs were just show dogs or trial dogs and were of little or no use when it came to a day's work. Of course in those days anything they said was right and that was my lead.

But through working, training, and selling dogs, my interest grew and I started to go watch trials. The more trials I attended, the more I learned, not only about training, but also about dogs: their strengths, their weaknesses, what I liked and what I did not. Going up this path, I did as many wrongs as I ever did rights, but for me looking back, it was a tremendous learning experience and one to this day I still credit. It took me into the registered dogs, which in

The dog relaxing and thinking as he gives freedom to the sheep.
*Photo by Tom Moates.*

turn made everything easier.

I would watch the dogs I liked and listen to others to hear their opinions. It was something that fascinated me, and I would try to get to as many trials as I could during this time. Of course it was all as a spectator, but the benefits, the experience, and the leads gained are beyond words. A quote from a top handler back then was, "If you want to know answers, go ask the good handlers, but if you want to do what I did, go watch them." I still think of that statement today and for me how true it is. Too many people today want to be told how, and through lack of try, never learn through their failure. A mistake corrected is by far your best answer, likewise for your dog. Sometimes for me, looking back on those times are still special and even now can still make answers come easier. It's when looking back on where I come from that gives me the insight on what these dogs, if given a chance, can teach us. Oh, I know, we think we are the teacher, but really for me it's the other way around. Like everyone else, I started out thinking I knew all the answers, but the more years I have put in, as I study dogs, their answers far surpass mine. Many of the mistakes and struggles I have made over the years could have been avoided if only I had studied and understood my dogs, but instead I felt I knew, and in the process they had to do it my way. I give lots of credit to the opportunity I have had through clinics and seminars I have been honored and privileged to put on. The challenges they gave and the answers that were needed. It still amazes me, each clinic I put on, how when given the chance these dogs have so much more to give and show us if only we can be patient enough to wait and give them the chance. The dogs, as they show the answers, not only teach me about how to relate to them, but teach me more and more on how to accept and enjoy my life in general.

So how can we give back to the dogs the rewards, the strengths, the feelings, the respect, they so much thrive on? I think we start with respect for what they give us. Say the mistakes they make, let's try to understand why, and then help the dog with the problem rather than make it right. In the process we allow our dogs to use their minds and with our help come up with their own answers, which in turn, they deliver back to us. This builds their confidence and respect for us. Dogs, to me, love to give rather than be made. Let's look at judging, trialing, training, it's all about what we want not what our dogs need. I watch, listen, and see rules changed, sheep trained for the trial, water on the trial field, training fields for our dogs and wonder, "why?" My answer is to make it easier or an excuse for doing things the wrong way. I understand that sheepdog trialing has changed and as a good friend of mine once said, "It's a commercial business in this day and age." Well, maybe for some, but for me, I am, I guess, old fashioned.

Let's start with judging and the changes we have made and want to accept. Are they to help our dog, make it easier for us, or maybe just an excuse? I think the answers are free to how each individual wants to use them, but here are some of the answers I come up with. As one walks onto the trial field and reaches the handler post, his or her dog has already spotted the sheep and is ready to go. The dog may be 20 feet or so from the handler and in many cases, too far away from the handler's feet to satisfy the judge, but for me here is a dog going onto the course thinking for himself, poised, and ready to go. I ask, why would we want to penalize a dog who in my opinion, has scoured the field, spotted the sheep, and is at the ready? The only answer I come up with is because of the handler who follows, goes to the post, and deliberately sets his dog up a distance away to try help the dog find his sheep. As a judge, I feel I can tell the handler who tries to cheat and would penalize him accordingly. I see little advantage to having our dogs be within five or six feet of the handler before being sent. It's the same for me with dogs that are set up to go off square. Too many handlers today are making the outrun on their dogs rather than correcting the wrong. If we penalize the wrong we will be helping handler and dog in the process. Allowing handlers to use distance to make dogs find sheep or land right at the top does not help our dogs.

It's the same on the lift. Too many dogs are not stopped at the top because we fear they may struggle lifting. It's the part of the course where sheep can be made but we must go back to judging lifts the correct way. Outruns and lifts carried out in the right manner, build feel and trust between dog and sheep. Again, if we were tougher on judging here we would see sheep change. We often blame our sheep, but seldom ask why. It's the same on our fetch and drives. It's all about lines and hitting gates, in other words, flanks and stops rather than pace and control, but it's the pace and control which is going to give the best answer to the dog that has feel and balance.

The handler's post is another place. Many people encourage moving away from the post to make it easier for the dog, but it's the test we should want not the easy way. Again, the test will prove the better dog. As I have already mentioned, the post is where the handler stands. The sheep should be brought around one's feet. The pen and the shed are other great places to test our dog's balance, feel, and power, but only if judged the correct way. We can only help our dogs be good if we judge the way it should be. Tough judging will be the answer to better dogs.

Training sheep for the trial is another practice I do not agree with. Trained sheep only make the job easier, or so they say. I have seen sheep which were supposed to have been trained, and I would rather they had been left alone. We don't make good sheep; it's freedom and feel that takes fear away. Most of the time, while people think they're training sheep, often they are adding fear. Sheep are like a dog or a person; they never forget, especially the fear part. I understand the principle of trying to have better sheep for trials, but certainly don't feel it helps us have better dogs.

It's the same with water on the course. People want bigger and tougher courses to find the better dogs, yet because of the heat we need water on the field for our dogs. What I feel is, we don't need a huge course to find the good dog. We need to control sheep in the right manner around the course, so that sheep and dogs alike have a fair chance to show their respect and feel for each other. I don't know about others, but for me, when I go to buy a dog I don't need a huge field to study and look for his talents or weaknesses. Look at our dog sales today. No big courses but unbelievable prices.

Practice fields before a trial, again, not for me. I honestly believe that for a dog trained the correct way with a handler who trusts and respects his dog, a practice field is the worst place to go. Dogs, sheep, and people are all alike when we are given the chance to think as we are taught. The chances of forgetting are pretty slim. Sometimes when I think about trialing, we are so busy trying to make everything better, yet if we looked at our wrong and corrected our mistakes, our whole answer is already there.

# Chapter 29:

# Ettrick Kennel

In 1975 I moved to Wisconsin where I went out on my own and started putting together Ettrick Kennels. This meant a trip to Scotland for about five weeks to spend with family and friends. Plus I wanted to try to buy the kind of dogs I needed to put together a kennel that someday I would be proud to own. The name "Ettrick Kennels" came from the valley I used to live in and love.

Many good memories come from my time in Ettrick. Times I will always remember and treasure, hence the name Ettrick became my kennel name. Buying dogs to start my kennel did not come easily. Money was tight, and although I ended up with seven dogs, they were maybe not as good as I would have liked, but as good as I could afford at that time. Since then, it has been my ambition to add and build the name Ettrick Kennels to where, not only the public would notice, but to what I would expect, feel proud, and give honor to the name of Ettrick. It has been a fun and challenging journey.

There is still a long way to go, but I feel good about where we are.

Over the years many dogs have been added and gone, with the one thing in mind, I have never seen the best so I will always keep looking. Dogs who have come in and help build the kind I want to represent the kennel, have to please me. I have a saying, "If its not good enough for me it's not good enough for my customers."

Looking back on dogs that I brought in, I had a bitch named Joy that went back to Gordon Rogerson breeding. She was a dog that bred well, leaving the type of pups that grew into the kind of dogs I was looking for. Another was Nell, an older female I acquired from R. Henderson, and another from R. Henderson named Meg, and Jill, a Johnny Wilson dog—all early dogs who for me started to form my kennel.

As time went on I strived to advance, spending more money to try to find the better dogs that turned me on, dogs that were to my liking, with something in them I would see and I thought would strengthen the operation. Dogs like Alex Waugh's Jed, Bill Elliot's Jan, George Scott's Maid, and Aled Owens' Meg were all top females that added quality to our kennel.

On the male side, we've had dogs like Dryden Craig, Kathy's Bob, and Jake, who was to father many fine dogs as well as place high in the trial circle. Credit to building my kennel name has to go to some great friends and people I owe much to in the help they gave; the advice and information I received while trying to find the quality dogs that has built Ettrick Kennel into what it is today. It may not be full of winners, but for me its full of quality, something I see missing and disappearing in our dog world today.

It's a dangerous place to go but I feel it would be wrong not to mention some of the people who have meant so much to me in my search for success. Starting at the top is my long time friend and buddy, the late Johnny Wilson. I could write a book on John and me, the ups, downs, fun, the laughs, but the main part was that it was a very special connection, one I treasure and respect. Johnny, his wife

May, and their family have been very special for me not only because of the dogs and who Johnny was, but because they are considered as part of my family.

Others at the top of the list are Paul and Irene Turnbull from whom I have bought many good dogs and stolen lots of good advice, although they may not know it.

Above all and very special when it comes to friends: Aled Owen and his wife Jano. It's hard to believe sometimes how friendship develops. It's an interesting story how Aled and I met, one that I feel was meant to be. I was doing a clinic in New Mexico, and a lady named Betty Maddox had a dog named Rex that caught my eye. It was a dog that she had imported from Aled. Another lady had a female named Nell that was by Jim Brady's Jim, and I said, "If you should ever breed the two I would be interested in a pup."

A year later they called and said they had a pup for me, hence Bill became an important part of my kennel. I was so impressed by my pup that I decided I wanted to see more of that line which traced back to Aled's Ben, another dog that impressed me, although I only had seen him on video. That summer we went home to Scotland and of course my first visit was as usual to see Johnny Wilson. We had been out and saw some dogs work and returned to the house for coffee. I was telling Johnny that for all the time I lived in Scotland I had never been to Wales, but that I was going to try to go and see more of Aled's Ben line.

About the time I finished telling Johnny this, there was a knock at the door and unbelievably it was Aled, who never had been to Johnny's before. He and two friends had come to Scotland on a trip to see dogs and dropped by to see Johnny. As we told him the story about me wanting to go down to Wales and see his dogs, no one could believe the coincidence. Aled asked me to go down. I did. We spent two days, and another friendship was formed. I have bought many dogs from Aled through the years, and the friendship I have built with Aled and his family is another treasure I owe to these dogs.

Last, but not least, are my good friends Andrew and Francis Dickman. I have bought many dogs through Andrew, dogs that were to help build Ettrick Kennels. There are too many to mention all of them, but two tops were Kathy's Jake and My Jim. Kathy's Jake was to bring fame, as well as breed many of the kind that makes us proud of the kennel name. My Jim I saw at six months and said to Andrew, "If you ever sell him I would like first chance." I got Jim as a three year old and felt in myself he was one of the best I ever owned. Jim won much for me but was bred to very little. He was a dog that I studied a lot and never knew why he wasn't used for breeding. Jim had all the things I like to see in a good dog. Again, my friendship with the Dickmans started out through the dogs but the friendship overlapped everything the dogs had to offer. They have been loyal, honest, and above all the best friends one could ever hope to have.

There are many others who are looked up to, and I hope they do not feel left out because it's you, the friends, the students, and your dogs that have helped make this all possible. It's with your help that Ettrick Kennel is what it is today. My goal has been and continues to be to breed the type of dog that catches my attention, which in turn will improve the dogs being used for breeding at Ettrick Kennels.

# Chapter 30:

# Family

Writing this book has been challenging for me, but the biggest challenge was what to write about people. When I first set out, I had in mind to tell stories of many of the great handlers I have met, of friends who have meant so much—yes, people who I believe could have made an impact on my book. But after many tries I decided that it could be a wrong idea. It's not that there were not great tales to tell and answers to gain, but after great thought, I decided to leave that side alone as I believe these people should be left to tell their own stories. A decision now I am glad I made.

However, there are a few people I must give credit to. I was born in a family of seven children, with three brothers and three sisters. At the age of two, I lost my Mother. As one can well imagine, for me it was something I have no memory of. I only know it was something I would have treasured, and in some ways do. I know she was a great woman, and at times I feel torn at what I missed. However, I had a family who made up for most of it. My eldest sister, Jean, then came home at age seventeen years and gave up her whole life to devote her love and honor to raise us kids. I often think what that must have meant as she stayed home and kept the family and home together for the rest of her life. Of course I was her little boy, and I will always be grateful for what she gave and how she gave it. These had to be hard times. My father was a farm worker, earning an average wage, raising seven kids, plus having to find a little extra for sister Jean.

I suppose many think of their fathers as great, but for me, mine was a model to follow. Much of what I do today with dogs comes from the way he raised me. I never remember my Dad being angry, and yet he was always in control of us kids and the people around him. It took little to please him, and his work was his enjoyment. I never remember getting a spank from my father, not that there weren't times when I needed it, but if my Dad was unhappy, I was usually the same or crying because I had upset him. My respect for Dad was something that has brought me a long way in life. When I played sport, or did anything for that matter, he taught me to accept the correction and would say, if you can't accept you don't need to play. That is something I feel is right to this day. My Father left many answers and gifts for me in his life, the kind I want to pass on to you and especially my dogs.

I will never forget the last time I saw my Father. He had a stroke four years prior to that in which he lost his voice. Through all that time, he never showed emotion. In fact, I never remember seeing my dad cry. As a child, I am sure he would hug me, but as a grown up it was a handshake, one which was meant. All the time he was in hospital, and through that last four years, the doctors said that his mind was so that he did not understand. But I did not believe it. On my last visit home, we would go see him every night with one or others from the family. On my last night I asked to go alone; I don't

Jack's oldest sister Jean who raised him after his mother's death. Jack
is on the right with George, two years older, on the left.

know why but I did. It's a night I will feel and remember for the rest
of my life. We sat and I talked. I would say things and he would
nod or squeeze my hand. I knew in some way that he was trying to
tell me something, and by the end I had my answer; it was a wrong
I had done and he wanted me to know it. I can remember getting
up to leave and for some reason knew that this was the end. I held
his hand, said good-bye, and left with upset feelings. As I walked
down the corridor something said, "you have to go back." When I
reached his room, he sat in his wheel chair sobbing. I ran up hugged
him and could tell he did not want to let go. Since that moment my
Dad is with me every day, never praising, but always there to help me
find an answer. To some this might not mean anything about dogs,
but for me it's where I got all my answers. Family is a wonderful
thing, something we at times take for granted.

One of the sadder times in my life was when my first wife Ann and
I broke up. It was hard to believe the pain and suffering it all caused.
Time passed and wounds healed, but I will never forgive myself for
the hurt it caused. On the better side, I have two daughters, both

Kathy, Kate, and Jack at Soldier Hollow enjoying a happy ending. *Photo by Anita Pratt.*

married, and four grandchildren; Jacqueline and Matt, who have Vivian and Glen, and Julie and Stuart with Evelyn and Finlay. I am a lucky man to have such a rich and loyal family, and blessed that we all get along.

As time passed, life moved on and it was then when I was to meet the one who was to change my life forever. Kathy came into my life through the dogs, at first helping to take care of them, then was offered the chance to train, and guess the rest is history. When Kathy first came, it was obvious to see her passion and love for the dogs; not only the dogs, but love for livestock. I could tell many stories from these early years, but the important one is the outcome and where it has led her. She is my number one student, who I did not teach. She taught herself with little or no guidance from me.

I can remember as she went up the ladder how she felt she would never make it, but make it she did! She moved up through training, trialing, and was the first woman to win the USA National Finals—we were married in 1984 and she won the title in Sheridan, Wyoming in 1995. That makes me the first man to win the finals and Kathy the first woman. I guess I could go on and on with

Kathy's achievements but the records talk for themselves. She is a top clinician, trainer, and trialer, who has only begun. Her strengths and goals stand out for me: she can read sheep, she teaches dogs to handle sheep with feel, taking away the fear and allowing animals to think. Kathy is good with people and has a way of conveying the message people want and need. Some people may think I taught Kathy, but I know Kathy can teach me.

A marriage is golden, but family adds the cream, and in 1999 Kate, our daughter, came into our world. Kate has added so much to our lives. To see Kathy and Kate, the happiness they have for each other fills and completes me; these are the things, to me, that family is all about. To you, Kathy, Kate, my family and friends, thank you for guiding and making me into who I am. Thank you for giving me a life filled with richness and allowing me to leave my rights and to correct my wrongs.

# *Afterword*

It's funny to look back and see and feel all the changes that have been passed on to me by these dogs and by you folks, the owners of the dogs. It's been a lifetime of change, experience, fun, and, even today, learning. It's when I look back that I ask the question, "So where from here?"

There are many answers: the "what I want," the "what we need." Is it the glory, the success, the fame? What is it, I ask myself, that keeps me going? What gives me the enjoyment and chances to do what I do with people and dogs?

At times, I'm even amazed myself at many of the answers we can come up with. The answer for me is simple: it's the dogs and the challenge they give. It's not so much the challenge as the help they need to overcome it. This is where I find my answer. The dogs get their answer, and in the process, you, the dog owner, sees your answer. It is so much of this I find inside myself, my feelings, and where they want to take me.

The journey will be never ending because of the opportunities you and your dogs have given. The challenges they made and the answers I received are what made me who I am today. It's been the journey of a lifetime, one that I want to follow, carry on, and enjoy. To each owner and dog who has treaded my path I say a big, "Thank you!" And if the future can give as much as the past, my life and goals will be complete.

Jack after winning the Meeker Championship with Maid.

# *About the Author*

Jack Knox hails from Greenlaw, Scotland, a rural expanse in the Lammermuir Hills of the Scottish/Anglo border region, that region being the very namesake of the dog that has shaped Jack's life: the Border Collie. Jack is a celebrated herding dog trainer, renowned for his unique approach to training that cultivates a dog's intelligence and instincts to herd rather than tightly controlling a dog's movements. Jack's work with dogs brought him to the United States in 1971 where he has enjoyed a long, illustrious career that includes founding Ettrick Kennels, teaching herding dog clinics across North America, winning many dog trials including the USBCHA National Finals, and in 2003 being inducted into the America Border Collie Association Hall of Fame. Jack and his wife, Kathy, also a distinguished herding dog trainer, live in Butler, Missouri.

www.ingramcontent.com/pod-product-compliance
Lightning Source LLC
Chambersburg PA
CBHW020334100426
42812CB00029B/3117/J